JUDAISM AND CHRISTIANITY

*(based on the Charles William Eliot Lectures
at the Jewish Institute of Religion, New York,
1946–7)*

JUDAISM AND CHRISTIANITY

by

JAMES PARKES

LONDON
VICTOR GOLLANCZ LTD
1948

296
2092

Printed in Great Britain by
The Camelot Press Ltd., London and Southampton

To

DOROTHY

without whose constant encouragement
and co-operation these lectures would
never have assumed their present form

I WISH TO EXPRESS my profound gratitude to the Jewish Institute of Religion and to its President, Dr. Stephen S. Wise, for the invitation to deliver the Charles William Eliot Lectures in December, 1946, and January, 1947. Those lectures form the basis of the study of the relations of Judaism and Christianity, which are here published.

JAMES PARKES.

NEW YORK,
  January, 1947.

BARLEY,
  January, 1948.

TABLE OF CONTENTS

INTRODUCTION

THE MAIN THESIS of this book, the equal permanence and validity of the revelations of Sinai and Calvary, was first put to a conference of American Jewish chaplains in London in 1944. It was then enlarged into a series of four lectures delivered at the Hebrew University, Jerusalem, in the spring of 1946. The suggestions and criticisms made on those occasions were taken into further consideration when Dr. Wise invited me to deliver the Charles William Eliot Lectures at the Jewish Institute of Religion, New York, in 1946–7. These lectures in turn led to further discussions which have been embodied in the present book.

The experience which lay behind the lecture to the American chaplains lay not in the field of theological or New Testament studies, but in contact with modern Jewry and with Judaism. Had events not turned my attention to the problem of antisemitism and the situation of the Jewish communities of various parts of the world, I would in all probability have retained the views of Judaism, and particularly of Pharisaism, that I learned as a theological student and shared with the immense majority of my Christian contemporaries. But the study of antisemitism and of the Jewish world of to-day led inevitably to an examination of the long centuries of troubled history which lay behind, and alone explained, the ugly manifestations of hatred and defamation marking the political life of Europe of the nineteenth and twentieth centuries. And it soon proved impossible to understand the history of the Jews without some knowledge of the history and content of Judaism. It was in this last study that I moved into a world to which my New Testament studies had given me no key. A religion which had brought not merely power of survival, but a deep and overflowing tide of happiness and peace and of spiritual splendour to a people harassed beyond all others, was not the religion with which I had believed myself

familiar from the Christian commentaries on the Gospels
and the letters of St. Paul. A people who had shown the
power of creative co-operation with their neighbours
which nineteenth-century Jewry had shown once the
ghetto walls were down were neither the egotistical and
exclusive advocates of an arid legalism and exclusivism so
constantly described by modern theologians, nor the victims
of a divine curse so familiar in the pages of the Church
Fathers. The last stage of the process which had led from a
study of antisemitism to a study of Jewry, and from a study
of Jewry to a study of Judaism, led from a study of Judaism
to a re-examination of the sources of the Christian tradition
in which I had been educated.

That traditional view falls into two obvious divisions. It
had, in the first place, a clear picture of Judaism as a formal,
exclusive and legalistic religion which is a burden to its adherents, a picture which is repeated with complete consistency from the letters of Paul, or the Matthean denunciations of the Pharisees, down to the school books of the different Christian denominations of the twentieth century. It
would be otiose to seek to give examples; they are familiar to
every Christian student. In the second place, there is equal
consistency in the view of the Christian relations with the
Jewish people which results from this conception of Judaism.
The Christian task is seen to be simply and wholly contained
in the duty of converting the Jews to Christianity. It would
be pleasant to add, "and to secure justice for the Jews living
under Christian princes," but it would not be true. Even
to-day the section of the Churches concerned directly with
the missionary approach has taken no effective place in the
struggle against antisemitism; what they have done has
been confined to resolutions, and is naïvely revealed by the
minutes of their meetings to have been merely the product
of a feeling that a new tactical approach may secure better
results than they have hitherto achieved.

I do not know whether it be matter for praise or blame,
but the consequences of the re-examination to which I was
forced were not to undermine my Christian convictions or

my acceptance of the traditional Christian doctrine of the person of Jesus of Nazareth. On the other hand, I was led to a revision of the nature of the conflict between Jesus and Pharisaism, and, even more, to a reassessment of the nature of Paul's conception of the Law, and of his relations with Pharisaic Judaism after his "conversion." For the Judaism which had sustained Jewry during its long martyrdom was precisely that Judaism which was developed by the Pharisees of the Gospels, and was based on the Law of which Paul was held to be so violent an antagonist. For there is no evidence of any violent break between the teachings of first-century Pharisees and their rabbinic successors. The result has been a rejection of the Christian traditional interpretation of Paul, in spite of the distinguished line which runs from Augustine through Luther and Calvin to Karl Barth.

It may appear presumptuous to suggest a new line in any field so thoroughly examined by specialists as is that of the New Testament save in a work based on original material and heavily garnished with footnotes and references. But the material for a re-examination of the position of Paul is almost all to be found in two familiar sources. Either it lies in the New Testament itself, and in the decision between the letters and the last chapters of the Acts of the Apostles as the clue to the Pauline attitude; or it is to be found in the more recently examined pseudepigraphal literature of the period. For this enables us to see that some at least of the Pauline doctrines connected with the Messiah, which had appeared "un-Jewish" so long as we based our ideas of Judaism on the rabbinic Judaism which followed the Jabne reformation, were in fact adaptations of thoroughly Jewish ideas as held by sects and groups which disappeared from the Jewish landscape in the conflict with Rome and the Jabne reforms.

It was not therefore new manuscripts, but the Judaism of the Talmudic, medieval and modern Jewish communities which seemed to make this reassessment necessary. Judaism is no more the religion of the Old Testament than Catholicism is the religion of the New. Though both are rooted in the Bible, both have grown, under divine guidance, as the adherents of each believe, through many centuries of life and thought. The traditional Christian interpretation of Jesus and Paul implies that a quite definite subsequent development of Judaism was bound to take place. It had lost divine authority; its adherents were under a curse as a result of the crime of deicide; all truth had passed from it to the religion of Christianity, and in Christianity all the promises made to it were fulfilled and all its spiritual content was retained. The history of the last two thousand years dis-proves every one of these statements. If there are weaknesses in the history of institutional Judaism, there are weaknesses also in the history of institutional Christianity. If the hand of God is visible in the story of the Church, it is equally visible in the story of the Synagogue.

That is the standpoint from which this re-examination of the past and present relations of the two religions grew.

I would like to make clear at the beginning that, though I shall have much to say of co-operation between the two religions, I do not desire to undermine the integrity of either. A Christianity without the Cross is as emptied of meaning as a Judaism without Torah; and it is because a religion based on the Cross and a religion based on Torah, as each has historically developed, are to-day in any honest interpretation incompatible that Christianity and Judaism are rightly two religions. I do not regard Judaism as an immature Christianity, still less as a religion whose creative vitality and truth have ceased to exist. In this time and generation, not only do I not desire to see the conversion of all Jews to present forms of Christianity, but I do not seek the union of the two religions. That may happen in the future. But it can only happen when I can openly bring all that I value of the Christian tradition to the common pool, and the Jew can equally openly bring all that he values of the Jewish tradition. And that day is certainly not yet, and in our present circumstances a religion made out of patches and compromises and superficial syntheses would be a monster lacking the very qualities which give each religion its permanent value to humanity.

There is one final question to which it is, perhaps, appropriate to refer in this introduction. The book is inevitably addressed to both Jewish and Christian readers; and in each case there is the difficulty that each group is convinced that it understands the religion of the other. The Christian scholar, in assessing what I say about "the Law" in speaking of Paul, has in his mind a picture of "the Law" which he believes to be correct, and it is with difficulty that he can appreciate that it is, in most cases, a view which Jewish scholars would rightly regard as woefully inadequate. In the same way, Jewish scholars find it difficult to realise that the sincere Christian usually finds that even a sympathetic approach of a Jewish scholar to the person of Jesus and the basic tenets derived by Christian theology from its Christological doctrine entirely misses the point of what Jesus means to the Christian believer. That at least has been my experience, and my work has brought me more, and more intimate, contacts with Jewish believers of all kinds than falls to the lot of most Christian ministers.

This difficulty particularly affects the subjects of the first three chapters, where I shall sometimes seem to one side or the other to be labouring a point which is obvious, or evading the consequence of a deduction which is traditionally made by either Jew or Christian of the agreed historical facts. Such a difficulty is inherent in the subject once it is treated from the standpoint adopted of the equal validity of the two religions; for each has historically assumed to itself a greater measure of divine authority than it concedes to the other.

Part One

THE THESIS

CHAPTER ONE

JUDAISM AND CHRISTIANITY IN THE PURPOSE OF GOD

SINCE A TRUE UNDERSTANDING of the nature of Judaism and Christianity is not a matter of academic interest, but one vitally affecting the spiritual foundations of our present society, it is appropriate to start from some appraisal of the general enviroment in which such a discussion takes place, and an estimate both of the possibilities and responsibilities of religion at the present time.

Henry Wallace described the period into which we are entering as "the Century of the Common Man"; but the basic difficulty which we have to face is that only from a technical standpoint are there any signs that the common man is able to enter into this new heritage. We have scientific knowledge of all sorts, adequate to provide him with a good life. But we are no longer living with the nineteenth-century certainty that science can provide an answer to all the problems set by life. For life is not scientific, and we are slowly and painfully learning that it is not even rational. Unlike the nineteenth century, we have discovered that the emotions and the will form a trinity in man with his reason, and that, as in the Christian Trinity, none of these three is afore or after the other.

Once we begin to examine the problems connected with the emotions and the will, we are confronted with the whole issue of man as a spiritual being who needs both spiritual freedom and spiritual authority. But we have to deal with a wholly modern version of that problem. Owing to science and to our capacity for external organisation, the modern world is subjected to the possibility of authoritarian control in the interests of political power such as was never dreamt of by our ancestors; and the recovery of a spiritual power able to balance political power becomes not only even more urgent, but also even more difficult. In days when the village forge could produce the same weapons as those in the possession of the State, rebellion against intolerable authority could always seem, and often was, a viable alternative. In days when the power of extending propaganda was limited to that of the human voice or the printed word, the village agitator or reformer, and the secret publisher of pamphlets and manifestos, had almost the same power of making their views heard as the government or Church which they opposed.

To-day the problem confronting those who believe that progress without freedom is impossible is much more difficult. On the one hand, the need for a real power to balance the State is evident, and this power needs to rest on more than the repetition of noble principles, which the State itself easily uses for its own ends. But, on the other, the common man is an uncertain ally in the issue. His economic comfort and even his basic economic existence have become far more dependent on the smooth functioning of the vast machine of government than they ever were before. It will be easier than ever before to destroy the dissentient voice and to represent any opposition to the powers-that-be as a factious attempt to deprive the common man of his security and the good things of this life. More than one government has set out to repress "dangerous thoughts."

In this situation, there is one form of religion which authoritarian governments, aware themselves that men are neither mechanical nor rational, will tend to encourage; and that is a religion which abstains from concern with political and economic questions, and promises only what the Americans have wittily called "pie in the sky." But that is not a form of religion with which Jews, or Christians who are Protestants or, like myself, Anglicans, are or can be contented. For we are both concerned with our relations with a visibly disintegrating society, and with individual men and women within it; and we believe that the restoration of creative harmony, both in society and in the individual, can only come from freely creative relations between a free political and a free spiritual power. Moreover, we believe that this relationship covers all life as a unity. There are no departmental watertight compartments, save in the narrowest technical fields on one side or liturgical fields on the other. The democratic society is concerned with the spiritual welfare of its members, and a living Church needs freedom of criticism and operation in the fields of social and economic activity as well as in its own internal life.

From our point of view, therefore, we seek a creative tension between Church and State. The solution either of Roman Catholicism or of Communism—for though their contents are in violent opposition to each other these two solutions are identical—is inadmissible. For a State dominated by a Church, which is the solution which the Soviet Union has achieved and the Roman Catholic Church desires, imposes the same tyranny upon the human spirit as a society with a Church dominated by a State, and the situation is not altered if the Church admits certain areas of freedom to the State or the State to the Church.

One final factor is of the utmost importance. It is of twofold character. While an increasing number of our scientific and political leaders are aware that the basic problem of to-day is essentially, and in the widest terms, religious, this recognition has not reached the "common man," who is always a generation behind in his thought; but it is equally true that only the smallest minority of the leaders who see the problem as a religious one seek the solution in the religion offered by either the orthodox or the modernist (liberal or reform) Churches of to-day.

Such are the main elements in the background of the problem under consideration—the part which might be played by Judaism and Christianity in the coming age, if these two religions were to regain the influence which

they have undoubtedly lost. But, though I agree with the
verdict which I believe to have been justly stated in the
paragraph above, that the future does not lie with either the
orthodoxy or the liberalism which we have inherited, yet
I believe it to be of the greatest importance to consider
our past history, if we are to find the right lines forward.

In the next two sections of the book I shall attempt to
describe the original separation of Christianity from Judaism, the growth of a traditional attitude to Judaism and the
Jews, and the scattered evidence of the change of that
attitude. Throughout the long centuries during which the
Church controlled the situation, she created the legend
of Judaism as a dead religion, all of whose creative vitality,
as well as its divine calling, had passed over into the possession of her rival. During the same period the Jews were
presented as an outcast people justly paying the price for
the deicide which they had committed. Even to-day the
two pictures are only gradually in process of being changed.
Only gradually is it coming to be realised that Judaism
is still a living religion and that the survivors of Jewry
have the right to be reckoned as a people. There is still
much to be done on both counts. Above all, it still needs to
be recognised that the two facts are but two facets of one
single fact; the creativity of Judaism and the creativity of
the Jewish people is one creativity. And this remains true,
even in this secular period, when among "Jews" as among
"Christians" there is an increasing proportion of men and
women who refuse to accept a religion based on revelation,
or a faith embodied in institutions originally created for
days very different from our own.

I have done my best in those sections to present the
situation as factually and objectively as I could. But what
I have to say now can only be a purely personal interpretation of history, leading to a purely personal interpretation
of its meaning. I speak as a Christian, as one who believes
in the essential truth of fundamental Christian doctrines.
But in a sense I would speak also as a Jew. That is, I speak
on the basis of believing Judaism also to be true—as true

as Christianity. My position is, I admit, peculiar; but it is the only way in which I can interpret the meaning of history. Both religions are true; but they are also different religions. Neither is simply an incomplete form of the other; and I do not desire to see either disappear, even by conversion to the other.

The two religions do at least start from a common origin, the monotheism which was evolved by that branch of the Semitic people which found a home in Palestine more than three thousand years ago. The two essential characteristics of the one God which rabbinic Judaism and Gentile Christianity inherited from their common ancestry in Israel were that He was active and His activity was moral. He was a God who made possible—indeed, demanded—an "I-Thou" relation with His creation. And however we may alter, modify or develop our theology to-day in the light of our present knowledge, I believe that neither Judaism nor Christianity could survive on the basis that there was neither creative activity nor morality in the ultimate reality of the universe. In other words, we can abandon many of the words in which our ancestors, whether before or after the separation of our two religions, described their God, but we cannot cease to share with them the belief that He is, in the deepest sense which at any period we can understand, personal. We know that the word "personal" is inadequate. We can call Him supra-personal; but we can never call Him by any name which implies less than we predicate of personality. Moreover, it is this fact of believing in a God who is objective, personal and active that gives Judaism and Christianity the possibility, if they can seize it, of providing a power to balance the modern State.

Believing as I do that God is in the highest possible sense personal, I admit that I find no difficulty in the conception of a Divine Incarnation in the space and time of the history of His creation. Acceptance of the possibility of unprecedented action is one of the more obvious consequences of our belief in our own personality—except for those who are wholly determinists. All that we ask of such action is that it should be consistent with the personality of the actor, and that is all I desire to ask in relation to the interventions of God in history which have traditionally been accepted as the foundation-stones of both Judaism and Christianity, and which I denote by the two terms "Sinai" and "Calvary." I could not therefore accept any interpretation of Sinai which involved a permanent "favouritism" in the relations between the Creator and His creation, and I could not accept those traditional interpretations of Calvary which make its acceptance the basis of a distinction between eternal salvation for some and eternal damnation for the majority. But if there be an interpretation of those two events which is consistent with the universal responsibility of the Creator to the whole of His creation, then I see no reason to reject them on the grounds that they do not happen every week, or that, since they form no part of a series, it is impossible for science to classify and describe them. I believe that the theologian has as much right to say to the scientist, "Cobbler, stick to your last," as the scientist has to say it to the theologian, and that it will be no bad day for humanity when theology has sufficiently recovered its self-confidence and self-respect to say it both loudly and clearly. For the superstition of scientists is really quite intolerable! That, however, is a digression.

If the fundamental relationship of Creator and creation is an "I-Thou" relationship—if, in other words, the development of this particular world depends on free and full co-operation between Creator and creation—then the evidence for Sinai and Calvary must be that these events spring out of the needs and possibilities of that co-operation. They must be consistent with what we can deduce of the purpose and method of the Creator; and they must answer some need of His creation which could not be answered in any other way.

In speaking of *the evidence* for Sinai and Calvary there is an important qualification to be made. By evidence I do not mean *proof*. There are no proofs or disproofs about the ulti-mate matters of the universe; there is only belief or disbelief in this or that hypothesis. But if there are no proofs, there is still a vast field in which it is possible to show that such a belief is reasonable or unreasonable, that it is consistent or inconsistent with our experience, either our personal experience or that record of our corporate experience which is history.

I seek, then, an interpretation of Sinai and Calvary which seems to me consistent with what I know of my own experience, and with my understanding of history. And this will mean there will be certain points which these two events share in common, since they are activities of one Creator, and certain that each possesses in unique measure by itself, since we have two events and not one.

The first common point to which I would draw attention is that they do offer an explanation of two historical phenomena, whose existence we cannot deny—the growth and survival of the Jewish people, and the growth of the Christian Church and its capture of the Roman Empire after three centuries, during which time it possessed neither military power nor government organisation. We cannot easily find real parallels to these events elsewhere. The second common point is that they are, much more than most important historical events, so unprovable that many persons of undoubted intelligence and probity refuse to believe they ever really "happened"; and that is extremely unusual of events which have left so important a mark on history. But I think it is also true to say that those who attempt to explain what undoubtedly has happened, i.e. that the Jewish people did survive and still do, and that the Roman Empire did adopt the Christian religion in the fourth century, without accepting the traditional view of why these events happened, find themselves in quite unusual difficulties. The attempt to explain the Church, while denying the historical existence of Jesus of Nazareth, has, in fact, been practically abandoned; but the Church is really just as difficult to explain on the basis of Jesus being an unusually good man. The dilemma of those who seek to explain Jewish history without accepting some unique event at Sinai can be seen, for example, by studying the learned but paralysing dullness of Oesterley and Robinson[1] and similar modern scholars.

They conventionally assert that Moses was the greatest man that ever lived. But, lacking belief (in their capacity as historians) in Sinai as a divine event, they have to explain this greatness otherwise. In one book they explain his eminence by stating that he introduced a section of the Jewish people to a thunder God who lived outside their own territory; and in another they proffer the alternative glory that he (temporarily) united some of the tribes into a single people. Truly world eminence can be easily gained!

The third common feature is the breath-taking audacity of the two events. If the traditional interpretation is correct, then the essential material for the spiritual development of mankind was entrusted in one case to a group of fugitive, homeless and obscure Aramean families, and in the other to a Galilean peasant. The figures given in the Old Testament narratives obscure the fact that the people whom Moses collected together and persuaded to leave the "flesh-pots of Egypt" cannot have numbered more than a few thousand families at most. At the time when they passed through the tremendous experience we associate with Sinai they were homeless wanderers, uncertain whether their more powerful neighbours would allow them to pass through their territory to find some place in which to settle. Compared with their neighbours their cultural development must also have been relatively low. They could not compare with the wisdom of Egypt, and it is doubtful if they even possessed the social cohesion and administration characterising the other peoples of the region. Likewise with the other "divine event." The longest period we can attribute to the ministry of Jesus of Nazareth is three years; and He died in his early thirties. The scene of His activities was an obscure province of the Roman Empire, possessing none of the cities which a Roman would have regarded as a centre of civilisation. This much then, can be said for them: there is no parallel in history to two such obscure happenings as the events leading to Sinai and Calvary, transmitting so enormous an influence to all succeeding generations.

I would say then that to me at least it fits most squarely with the historical facts which I know, to say that at Sinai and Calvary something happened which, so far as I know, has not happened in precisely that form on any other occasion in recorded history; and that that is why it is so difficult to prove them by ordinary methods. I believe that the relationship between man and God is continuous, that the spirit of God dwells in man, and that man finds his ultimate satisfaction only in communion with God. But on these two occasions there was, as it were, a spark between the terminals of "I" and "Thou" which made possible unique developments in space and time of this permanent communion with the Creator. In the latter case the event is adequately explained by the word "incarnation," but it ill fits the former; and we have no word which satisfyingly covers both. But rather than appear to give a lesser worth to Sinai, let me use the word "incarnation" to describe in both the bringing of something new into human history by the action on the stage of human history of its Creator. We do not know exactly what happened at Sinai, or how it happened; but there was born a conception of man working out the continuously revealed purpose of God in the life of a dedicated community which, judged by ordinary historical standards was, and still is, unique.

I believe it will be useful at this point to consider certain other interpretations of the significance of Judaism, especially as it is related to the separate existence of Christianity. There are two such of particular interest, one Jewish and one Christian, though neither have yet been completely translated into English. The first is that contained in a series of letters exchanged between Franz Rosenzweig and Eugen Rosenstock in 1916 and 1917, published by Edith Rosenzweig in 1935.[2] Rosenzweig still sees the particular mission of Israel to be the introduction of the world to pure monotheism, and here he is at one with a good deal of the thinking of Reform Judaism. There may have been something to be said for this so long as Judaism maintained that Christianity was not monotheistic. But that is not maintained either by Rosenzweig or by Reform Judaism. Their claim is only that Judaism is a *purer* monotheism. Now it seems to me, firstly, that it is an odd way for the divine activity to develop, to give the world the purer monotheism first, and the easier variant afterwards. I can see no reason for such a course. Secondly, I would deny that Judaism is a purer monotheism than Christianity. I think that in this case Jewish apologists have committed the sin so often committed by Christian anti-Jewish polemic. They have generalised from the worst, not the best, side of Christianity. There is Mariolatry, and there are doctrines of Christ as mediator which do separate the second and the first persons of the Christian Trinity, and these errors are very widespread. But they are not to be found in the serious theology of any of the great Christian Churches, which maintain the unity of God as strongly as ever did the Synagogue. Thirdly, I think it is a confusion between the pure monotheism of Judaism in itself, and the special qualities of Judaism as an element in a divine plan and purpose embracing the whole of history. No. That which is unique in Judaism among the religions of the world is its sense of a community as the vehicle for the fulfilment of the purpose of God. Since the emphasis is on *God* as well as on *community*, and, in fact, the purpose of the community is that the purpose of God should be fulfilled, it is natural that there should in Judaism be tremendous emphasis on the reality and unity of God. But equally because it is concerned with a community, Judaism is concerned with all sorts of things Christians have not recognised as being religious.

The second interpretation of Judaism is that of the Swiss Protestant minister, Leonhard Ragaz in *Judentum und Christentum*.[3] Ragaz recognises that Judaism is concerned with the community—with the Kingdom of God in this world. But, and here he is at one with a good deal of sympathetic Protestant thought, he sees the centre of Judaism in the prophets and not in the Law, so that his main interest is in the constant proclamation of the principles of the Kingdom as they are to be found in the prophetic writings. Undoubtedly modern Christian social thinking is more attracted to the prophets than to the books of the Law; but I believe that Judaism is right in seeing in the prophets commentators and auxiliaries of the Law, and not in any sense a substitute for it, or an improvement on it. For the essential characteristic of Judaism is not its lofty generalisations, but its attempt to devise the practice by which the Kingdom is actually built.

The modernist scholars of the nineteenth century uttered a great cry of joy when the code of Hammurabi was discovered (its complete text was first published in 1902, but much was known before that). They felt that they had got rid of any divine activity at Sinai for good. For Hammurabi antedated Moses by half a millennium. It is true that there is much in the code which Moses may have adopted. But the differences are more striking, as well as much profounder, than the similarities. There are no laws in the code of Hammurabi of which the sole sanction is: "for I am the Lord thy God." Likewise when the hymns of Akhenaton were discovered, there was another cry of joy that once again the Pentateuch was set down from its high position. The hymns of Akhenaton are, indeed, charmingly spiritual. But they suggest no laws as to the mutual responsibility of day-to-day life in a community. They forbid one neither to covet nor to steal.

I may be asked here: do you ask us to accept the whole Pentateuch as a document given by God to Moses? My reply would be: No. Sinai and Calvary are not isolated events, but events which are continuously active in the whole of subsequent history. I am not more concerned to prove that any part of the Pentateuch was given to Moses than I would be to prove that any of the Gospels were written by Jesus of Nazareth. The late Archbishop of Canterbury, William Temple, once said: "Revelation is always an event; it is never an interpretation. The task of interpretation is man's." Just as I believe the Gospels to be the attempt of first and possibly second generation Christians to set down the record of the tremendous experience through which they had passed, so I accept the Pentateuchal legislation as the attempt of successive generations to put into effect the tremendous experience first communicated to them at Sinai. The final act of Sinai was not any particular law or laws, but the affirmation of the people as a community: "All the words that the Lord hath spoken will we do."[4]

The new truths which constitute the Sinaitic revelation, though all were certainly not declared at Sinai, can be summarised under five headings:

1. The acceptance of a life which looks outward to the world, because it looks inward to God. That which is declared in the first commandment is the ultimate sanction on which are built the relations of men with men. An excellent example of the implementation of this is the commandment in Lev. xix. 34, where the sanction of the protection extended to the stranger is: "I am the Lord your God."

2. The life which turns thus outward and inward is a unity. Daily life is concerned with fulfilment of the will of God. There is no division of the field between "secular" and "religious." Man, even as a sinner, still lives in the City of God, for there exists no place else in which he could live.

3. Men live in community, and it is in community that they fulfil the will of God, not by the constant repetition of noble principles, but by the framing of just laws, by the training of honest and humane administrators, by the practice of neighbourliness and good citizenship and in a thousand practical and even technical ways.

4. There is no viable law for man or society except it be the law of God. It is here that we get the essential need for the doctrine of growth and interpretation which later separated Pharisees and Sadducees.

5. There lies on each living generation the responsibility for interpreting the will of God for its own times. It cannot

rest on the interpretations of its predecessors, even on the written word of Torah, for God speaks directly to each generation, in accordance with its particular needs, and in answer to its particular problems. Here is the background of the whole Talmudic system, and, beyond the Talmud, the Responsa of the Middle Ages.

From the historical standpoint, it is the last three which are the most peculiar to Judaism. Without them it is not possible to understand its survival, and it is the failure to understand them which has led so many centuries of Christian theologians, including those of the twentieth century, to talk so much nonsense about "the traditions of the elders." A religion which is concerned not only with eternal and unchanging verities (though I believe that even these need reinterpreting more often than the Churches allow), but with the daily life of a society, must have *as a quite fundamental doctrine* interest in practical, political and social details and provision for constant revision. Only so can religion avoid becoming reactionary and obstructive, and religious leadership maintain communal leadership. So far from meriting the strictures of the conventional New Testament scholar, the doctrine of "the tradition of the elders" is one of the landmarks of human progress. It dates, apparently, from that almost unknown period between the return from exile and the Maccabees to which is given the name of the "men of the great Synagogue," and it is not their only epoch-making discovery. The other is the fact that human nature is changed and human habits altered, not by periodic but irregular outbursts of the highest poetic and spiritual significance, nor by the presentation of the loftiest moral generalisations, but by a regular routine of systematic teaching, much of which will seem detailed and petty. Much Christian praise of the prophets, and much of Reform Judaism's love of lofty ethical generalisations, ignores the fact that it was the ancestors of the Pharisees and the rabbis who not only rescued the texts of the prophets from obscurity, but created a national community lovingly but laboriously committed to the task of embodying their teaching in their daily lives.

There is not a single verse of the New Testament which presupposes the existence of idolatry amongst Palestinian Jews. But it was not the prophets and their denunciations which eliminated it.

The new contributions of the Tannaim[5] and their successors were as striking as those of the "men of the great Synagogue." The first was the system of reinterpretation by continual discussion, and not by the periodic summoning of a council of men, however eminent or holy. Here is a discovery which in the realms of science and economics men have just begun to make at the beginning of the twentieth century, as they show by the foundation of research institutes in which men continually work together in teams. But the religious world still satisfies itself with the occasional council or conference, with inadequate time and overcrowded agenda.

The second was the doctrine of intellectual responsibility. It is probably true to say that the *system* of intellectual argument evolved by Talmudic scholars is inferior to that of the philosophers of Greece, and that it easily became somewhat arid and rigid. But that is not the question. There are many sayings in the Talmud which, curious or fantastic in themselves, yet reflect the basic belief that it is man's business to understand the will of God, and that man can do so, and must do so, not allowing even respect for God to interfere.[6]

The third is the complementary recognition of the many-sidedness of truth, and our inability with imperfect knowledge to reconcile all opposites. The Bath Kol's decision between one rabbi and another is an example of it.[7] But any professor who has Jewish students in his class has had innumerable examples of this. The Hellenistic-Christian system of thought presupposed one authoritative answer to one question, and the common acceptance of the verdict of authority. The Jewish system rather lauds the variety of interpretations which can flow from the same truth, and demands conformity only for practical reasons. Here is the essential and necessary basis of religious freedom combined with discipline.

The tragedy of Judaism was the gradual loss of vitality in interpretation, and this can only fairly be considered in relation to external pressures on Jewry. But coupled with that loss are two factors within the system of interpretation (for which Judaism also cannot be blamed), and which had an important effect on the Jewish religion.

The first is the loss of responsibility in the political field. A religious system such as is described in the preceding pages should reach its culminating point in the ordering of a free national life, and in the adjustments of a free community to its free neighbours. This rabbinic Judaism never experienced—and I may add that the deepest argument for the autonomy of the National Home lies in the making good of that lack. Jews individually in their emancipated life in the modern Western world have shown that the social virility of the Jewish tradition is dormant rather than destroyed. But that is only a partial substitute for control of communal Jewish development in a Jewish environment.

The second is complementary to the first. It is the doctrine that the law of the land is law. This may have had to be accepted as a political necessity, though it may also have been used to support a timid compliance in certain circumstances. But it is well to recognise that it was a tragedy, and resulted in the necessary Jewish acceptance of conditions both more primitive and more unjust than rabbinic law would have evolved.

It is the combination of these two points which led to that aspect of Talmudic teaching which both reformed Jews and Christians—often with equal lack of understanding—deplore; its interest in points of the minutest detail. There is nothing fundamental which can be said against the basis of this teaching. It is as good to seek and obey the will of God in the smallest matter as in the greatest, and there is equal joy in its fulfilment. The tragedy lies in the fact that minds which should have been occupied in the loftiest, most searching and widest issues confronting a national community, had enough time to deal with such matters, because they were precluded by their position from dealing with the other.

But the final tragedy of rabbinic Judaism was the application of the conception of a canon, with its inevitable closure, to the Talmud itself. A canon of Scripture is a serious enough matter. A canon of finality in interpretation denies the fundamental value of a doctrine of interpretation. For centuries Jewish life has suffered from the adherence of its orthodox leaders to the belief that no law can now be radically altered because no court can now be summoned conforming to the standards laid down by a Talmudic authority.

From the foregoing pages it might seem that there was nothing left to be said for Calvary and Christianity. But all that is predicated of the truth and the continuing validity of Sinai, I claim also for Calvary. I would begin by saying that I use the word "Calvary" as a symbol of the whole life and death of Jesus of Nazareth. The distinction between the two revelations lies not in the sphere of a purer or a less pure monotheism, nor, in spite of a good deal of Christian teaching, in the distinction between an affirmative and a negative attitude to this world. It lies in the complementary, not contradictory, sphere of the individual. That highest purpose of God which Sinai reveals to men in community, Calvary reveals to man as an end in himself. The difference between the two events, both of which from the metaphysical standpoint are identical as expressions of the infinite in the finite, of the eternal in the world of space and time, lies in the fact that the first could not be fulfilled by a brief demonstration of a divine community in action; but the second could not be fulfilled except by a life lived under human conditions from birth to death.

Though I recognise Judaism and Christianity as two religions, and two different kinds of religion, yet I can only recognise in Sinai and Calvary two closely interlocked and complementary stages of the unfolding of a single divine plan. I cannot carry our present separation from history back to God! The two religions are a historic fact; their

separation is not a divine intention. The relation of the two
revelations is twofold.

If, in the first place, we consider the life of Jesus, and
His teaching, it is concerned with the true way of life of the
citizen within the Sinaitic society. Much is made in Jewish
apologetic of the distinction between Jewish justice and
Christian altruism. There is, for example, an interesting
essay on this by Achad ha-Am,[8] in which he attempts to
show the greater excellence of the Jewish standard. I think he
is wrong. If a society is to be *just*, it will be because its members are *generous*. If the members themselves limit their
personal standards to justice, their corporate expression
will be a little less than justice. I see the failure of Christianity
in so many fields as results of its failure to recognise that the
personal ethics of the Sermon on the Mount fit like a hand into
a glove into the society of the Sinaitic revelation; because
that society fundamentally places personality above property. But they have never fitted, and will never fit, into the
Roman conception of society on which Christendom was
actually built. For that society places property above
personality.

From the very beginning Calvary presupposes Sinai. The
life of Jesus could not have been spent, nor the teaching of
Jesus given, in any other environment than that of the
Jewish community. The Jewish society, and Jewish values,
are presupposed in everything He said or did, presupposed
so completely, assumed so naturally, that no open reference
to them is necessary. What He had to say about God and
man would not have been understood in any other environment; long explanations would have been necessary; a
whole theological structure would have needed to be reared
as a framework on which men could have understood His
meaning—just as His followers found from the first that they
could not transmit His teaching to the Gentile world without
building up a theological doctrine of His person to make it
comprehensible. On the background prepared for Him by
the continuing creativity of Sinai, Jesus was able to proceed
to the second stage of the divine plan, the full revelation of

the nature and possibilities of the personality of man, and to demonstrate it not only in His teaching but even more in His life. That is the first link.

But from the Christian standpoint we have to consider, not only the life and teaching of Jesus, but also His death. Now although in its attitude to the Law the Christian Church has never understood the Old Testament, yet there is an aspect of the Old Testament which the Church has better understood than the Synagogue, and that is the place of sacrifice in man's religious life. Sacrifice is not peculiar to Judaism. It exists in some form or other in all religions. There is undoubtedly an element in the primitive doctrine of sacrifice for which the rabbis rightly substituted repentance and forgiveness, and the substitution was spiritual gain. But that is only one side. For the other there is no substitute. It is known traditionally as the doctrine of "vicarious sacrifice"; and it is a tragedy that the very unspiritual forms in which it has been put forward at various periods of Christian history, and in various schools of Christian theology, have made most modern theologians chary of using the word, and chary even of expressing the idea.

The belief underlying it is, in fact, not only profoundly spiritual, but it is an essential part of the relation of man to man in the unity of humanity and the relation of imperfect man to his perfect Creator in the unity of creation. It is a double idea. In the first place, there is the actual fact that repentance cannot undo the actual ill that has been done. If a man is killed, the man is still dead, though his slayer repent. Something has still to be put right which man cannot put right. A responsibility has to be accepted which man cannot accept. Primitive man felt this and sacrificed something he treasured to act as compensation. If it was an object, there was the weakness in the offering that it only created another deficit in the creation considered as a unity. If it was a living thing, whether animal or human, there was the further weakness that the actual sacrifice, the sacrifice of life itself, was involuntary. The symbolism of the scapegoat shows that part of this idea is embodied in Old Testament thought and was carried on in various forms of rabbinic orthodoxy; the series of "servant poems"[9] in the great prophet we call the Second Isaiah shows a far deeper appreciation of the problem. For there the sacrifice is voluntary as well as vicarious. But even that leaves unsolved the problem raised by Job, the problem of the unmerited suffering with which the universe is filled. The last words of Job are magnificent, but not final:[10] "I know that Thou canst do everything and that no thought can be withholden from Thee. Therefore have I uttered that I understood not; things too wonderful for me which I knew not. I have heard of Thee by the hearing of the ear; but now mine eye seeth Thee. Wherefore I abhor myself and repent in dust and ashes." It is a superb answer and the only one that could then be given. But it does not solve the problem of unmerited suffering. It only refers it back to God. And Christianity proclaims that God accepts this reference back. For to the Christian the answer of God is given on Calvary. The ultimate answer which primitive men and their successors sought in their many developments of the doctrine of sacrifice can only be given by the acceptance of responsibility for the sins, failures and sufferings of creation by Him Himself who created the conditions in which those sins and failures and that suffering inevitably occur. In Sinai God guides men to the way of life He had planned for them; in Calvary He makes atonement to men for all that the most perfect community cannot remove in the life of His creation. In the two together His relation with His creation is complete, and the unity of creation is restored.

If I were asked to what unquestionable historical fact I would point to justify my claim that in Calvary, as in Sinai, there was a divine event, I believe that the only satisfying answer would be in pointing to the emergence of a new type of human character and a new breadth of human experience expressed in those whom the Church calls saints. This is the field in which one would expect to find the evidence, for Calvary is personal as Sinai is communal

BJC

in its creativity; and it is out of a new evaluation of the person that the Christian saint emerges. That which Christianity affirms of the person of man, in its paradoxes and its challenge, seems to me to warrant such a claim for Calvary —though it may be well to repeat what I have said earlier, that this is a field in which there is no such thing as proof in the scientific sense. But at least it appears to me undeniable that the Christian claim about human nature is preposterous on any humanistic interpretation, and has its only justification in its belief in the birth into this world through Calvary of a new outflowing of divine power. I want to state this Christian belief, as far as I can, in its traditional orthodox form, and not to try to find words which would water down its paradoxes or its intimate relationship to a theological pre-supposition; because I believe that its full appreciation is essential to the further understanding that at present Judaism and Christianity are two kinds of religion, and that any superficial attempt at a synthesis would be disastrous to both. When I come to deal with Paul I shall argue that the essential Paul was the Christocentric mystic; and the recognition of this is fundamental, because it is Paul the mystic, with his eyes wholly concentrated on the meaning of human life once it is possessed by Christ, who made the first great contribution to this new understanding of man; and this understanding remains essential to all Christian reinterpretations, even if we strip all other Pauline views from our theology as outworn. This Christian doctrine of man, as the Chrstian sees him in and through Christ, can be resumed in five postulates:

1. Man is of infinite worth before God. To enable man to fulfil that part in creation for which God had designed him, God became incarnate in Jesus and died upon the Cross.

2. Man has infinite responsibility before God. To this end he is endowed with all his faculties and has been given free will. Through the abuse of these gifts there has come into the world sin, suffering, death.

3. This has given man a responsibility he can never meet. All that man can do by himself is insufficient to meet

his tremendous responsibility or restore what has resulted from his sin.

4. In the power of God, revealed and expressed in Christ, man can overcome his failures and achieve the perfection for which God designed him.

5. Man is an immortal being who is designed for eternal life in the eternal joy of fellowship with God.

It is from the Christian understanding of the meaning of the life and death of Jesus of Nazareth that these strange paradoxes as to the nature of man are drawn. Christianity, on the one hand, raises man to the highest dignity imaginable —man " for whom Christ died"; on the other hand, contemplating the immensity of the need which alone would justify such divine action, Christianity asserts with equal insistence the completeness and finality of human failure. It is at this fundamental level that there can be no truce with the humanist conception that man, by his own efforts, can attain his designed perfection. The Christian does not believe that it is true to the facts of our situation. It rests on a superficial interpretation of the place of evil in human history and in human nature. But there is a second paradox which flows from the Christian interpretation of the Incarnation. Christianity does assert that God calls men to perfection, and provides the power whereby they may achieve it. And then, as if terrified by the immensity of the claim it makes, it constantly lapses into the opposite extreme of being the most pessimistic and catastrophic of all religions.

Let it not be thought that I am denying to other religions the capacity to produce men in whom others recognise that peculiar quality which men accept as "saintliness." I am not even concerned in the impossible statistical task of finding out which religion could show the higher proportion of such individuals. Nor would I desire to make comparisons in terms of "better" or "more useful" between such individuals as a scientist giving his life and health to work in a laboratory for the alleviation of human suffering and a Father Damien giving his life and health among the lepers.

Paul himself is an excellent example of one of the new

types of character which flow from Calvary, the "fool for Christ's sake,"[11] giving the whole of his life and strength in a vocation which is itself new, the vocation of missionary. No century, no Church has lacked such men; and in most cases they have had a quality of universal appeal by which men of all faiths and characters have together seen in them something whereby their common humanity is made greater and more lovable. The contemplative, the ascetic and the theologian are other types of saint with which the pages of Christian history are filled. One feature which is remarkable, and to some extent applies to all the different types of saints impartially, is that they contain both men and women. No one could argue that the early Christians realised to the full the demands of modern women for complete emancipation; but there was never any hesitation in believing that the salvation which was offered in Christ was offered equally to women and to men; and there were famous women among the missionaries and mystics from very early times. And it was consonant with a new view of women that the extraordinarily vigorous, though almost wholly legendary, picture of the Virgin Mary, the "Mother of God," came into existence and played an important rôle in developing the tenderer virtues in the evolution of society. Christianity has often decayed in prosperity; it has never lacked its representatives, and women among the most noble of them, in the slum, the prison, and the hospital. Much social betterment has followed from such lives, but that was often an accidental by-product, with a tragic tendency to wither away once it required legislation or public action.

There is a second type of person who emerges into history at the same time as the saint—the cleric. The conception of the clergy and the recognition and enforcement both of their views and their authority by the secular State is something new, and still remains to all intents and purposes unique. But that the cleric, and the conception of the Church which he embodies, is part of the divine revelation of Calvary is something which I find myself increasingly unable to believe. This does not mean that I believe in an unorganised and wholly individualistic Christianity, but only that I cannot see in its present organisation that divine authority which the Catholic Churches—including my own —claim for it. Looking only at recent centuries and contemplating the terrible political activity of Rome since the Counter-reformation, and the equally terrible political inactivity of the Protestant Churches faced with the rise of nationalism and the industrial revolution, and in our own day Fascism and Hitlerism, I see no trace that here is something whose activity cannot be measured by wholly human yardsticks. Like other human organisations, the Churches have behaved sometimes better, sometimes worse, than contemporary corporate bodies making no such claims as theirs.

My insistence on the divine truth inherent in the Christian conception of the human person might appear to imply that what I am seeking with regard to the Jews is merely a novel form of conversionism, novel in the sense that I might seem to want to convert the Christians to a bit of Judaism in order to convert more easily the Jews to Christianity.

I do not believe such a policy to be right or possible. Both religions are conversionist, and both will and must stay conversionist. But as they are two different types of religion, so also they have two quite different types of conversionism, and so, in the foreseeable future, they must stay. The Christian religion is a mystery of salvation, and it converts by winning men singly to its life and teaching. Judaism is a way of life, and it converts by communicating some part of its way of life to the nations among which and within which it lives. Because of this difference the world, so to say, notices when a Jew becomes a Christian; and the convert must cease to be a Jew. But it does not notice when Jewish influence affects the political or social life of a Christian community, and the community itself does not notice that it has been in some respects converted to Judaism. Those are differences inherent in the situation which we cannot change, any more than we can change the fact that, if we do not accept traditional hypotheses which ascribe the whole truth exclusively to one side or the other, they must ultimately come together. But I do not believe that we can foresee such a period now, for neither side could accept the other without a loss which the other cannot replace.

A much more important and more actual question is: what is the contribution each of us can make to the world's present need, and part of that is concerned with our mutual relations. I think it is perhaps especially the Christian side which still has a great deal to do to see that the real nature of the religion of the Jews is fairly represented to Christian congregations. Too much seed ground is prepared for anti-semitism by bad Christian teaching. But likewise on the Jewish side there is still a tendency to describe Christianity as a less perfect form of Judaism.

Apart from that, I perceive the urgent task of each religion in the recovery of a new orthodoxy. I say "ortho-doxy" because I am convinced that the reform move-ments in each, while quite inevitable and indeed valuable contributions, have not yet found the way forward. To substitute the noblest generalisations for a concrete belief and a concrete discipline is to substitute a candle for a searchlight. But I do not believe that orthodoxy can regain influence so long as it claims for the interpretations of its divine events an infallibility which scholarship has not only disproved, but has the right to disprove. Traditional Judaism and traditional Chrstianity both belong in their formulations to a world which has passed, and which will not return. It is time we accepted that; and that we each continued and developed the meaning of those events whose early interpretations, whether in the Pentateuch or the Talmud, in the Gospels or in Patristic theology, rightly served their times, but will not serve us to-day. But the world has not yet found anything to replace what Judaism and Christianity might offer. Both alike proclaim belief in a God who is personal, active, intelligent and loving; and while

Judaism offers an exposition of true community, whether between men and men or between men and their Creator, Christianity offers a doctrine of man which in the range of its depth and height is adequate to embrace in one comprehensive sweep a Hitler and a Francis of Assisi. We need both Judaism and Christianity, for the sufferings of the present time are such that no explanation of them could be too profound or link too closely the whole fabric of the universe. In Judaism God says to man: fulfil My plan for creation; and man replies; I will. In Christianity man returns to God to say: fulfil that part in creation which I cannot because I am foolish and sinful; and God replies: I will. In Judaism and Christianity together the "I-Thou" relationship of a free creation is ultimately fulfilled. But in each is an essential part of the fulfilment, and until there appears the way by which they can fulfil the two together without losing their own essential nature, each must fulfil its own part. But the better the Jew or the Christian understands the reality of the religion of the other the better his own task can be fulfilled.

CHAPTER TWO

THE RELATIONS OF JESUS WITH THE JUDAISM OF HIS DAY

IN VIEW OF THE tremendous drama of their subsequent relations, we might naturally expect that the incompatibility between the teaching of Jesus and that of His Jewish opponents should have culminated in a clear-cut clash on fundamental issues and an obviously inescapable schism during the lifetime of Jesus Himself. Before the birth of modern scholarship, the Christian tradition indeed assumed such to have been the case, and to have been the cause of the Crucifixion. Nothing less seemed appropriate to the issues involved. But such a view is inconsistent with what is now increasingly recognised—that Jesus lived and died a Jew; and our present knowledge of Pharisaic Judaism enables us also to see that in the fundamentals of His teaching, in His message about the nature of God and man, about the kingdom of God, and about the relations of men to each other and to their Father in Heaven, there is nothing which does not stem from His Jewish background or is not to be found adumbrated in Pharisaism. The attempt to explain Him exclusively in terms of an earlier, prophetic, Judaism which Pharisaism had distorted and displaced, and to ignore the consistency of the long centuries of post-prophetic Jewish development, has been made impossible by the work of such scholars as Herford, Strack and Moore.

It might appear an escape from the new situation thus created to say that if the death of Jesus was not the inevitable result of a clash between His teachings and those of Pharisaic Judaism, then they were due to the particular wickedness

of the religious leaders of His day. But there is also a salutary
tendency to recognise that the events which led to His
rejection and condemnation involve our common humanity
and not the Jewish leaders of the first century alone; and
scholarship confirms that there is no evidence of any sudden
change in the nature of Judaism which would entitle us to
condemn it in the first century and yet recognise that in
subsequent centuries it fulfilled the divine task entrusted
to it at Sinai.

What is still to be realised is that those elements of base-
ness in the behaviour of the Pharisees which are to be found
in the Gospel narrative are irrelevant to the main issue,
and that the causes of the break lay in what the Pharisees
as well as Jesus saw of the truth. It is in differences of attitude
on points that will seem in themselves to be almost trifling
that the first stages are to be found which lead to the profound differences in the two religions. Yet somehow the
balance has to be retained which recognises the supreme
tragedy involved for Judaism in the rejection of Jesus;
but this can only result from the parallel recognition of
the second tragedy which followed later, when the followers
of Jesus rejected the real essentials of Sinai, a rejection
which has left the Church impotent in the face of the
breakdown of the modern world.

The statement that the issues between Jesus and the
Pharisees arose out of differences of attitude and points
which seem trifling does not mean that Jesus was otherwise
simply another Pharisaic teacher and that His mission was
to effect minor reforms in the Judaism of His day. Had the
followers of the two revelations not separated, there would
have been an entirely different story to relate of their effect
on the world during the two thousand years of their subsequent history. But, accepting the separation which has
taken place, we can say that it is so far from being true that
Christianity arises from minor reforms introduced by its
founder into Judaism that the significance of Jesus of
Nazareth in Christian theology would in no essential be
altered if we had no single record of His contacts with the

Jewish leaders of His day. In the whole of this chapter, dealing historically with His rejection and condemnation, we are touching but the fringes of the Gospels; the heart of Christianity is concerned with the positive message, and still more with the actual person, of Jesus Himself, and not with His controversies with the Pharisees.

There is one point which it is important to stress at the beginning of this historical enquiry, because it is too often forgotten when Christian scholars are examining Judaism, or Jewish scholars Christianity. No religion reveals its secrets to the purely rational and intellectual approach, however objective and scholarly it may be. At some stage even of an enquiry like the present, we must humbly accept that there are questions to which we shall receive no answer along the line of purely scientific or historical research. For if it is obviously wrong to teach, and equally foolish to believe, that which can be demonstrably shown to be false, yet there is a vast field in which the proofs and disproofs adduced by scholarship are irrelevant or at best inconclusive; and it is in that field that a religion makes its deepest impression on the human personality and its greatest contribution to human welfare. In its essence, religion is faith, faith which holds to hypotheses in realms beyond the reach of exact knowledge, because it finds these hypotheses are relevant to the actual business of living, and illuminate the problems with which the actual business of living is surrounded. It is important to remember this. It is not in mystical abstractions for the saintly few that religion passes beyond the realm of exact science, but in everyday life for the many; and it is in ordinary living that its hypotheses are most truly tested and most deeply held.

However deeply they disagree, the religious Christian and the religious Jew can understand one another. For both are at one in affirming that, though they have no secret doctrines which they desire to conceal from observation, there is such a thing as spiritual insight which is autonomous and governed by its own laws, and cannot be

apprehended by a scientific or purely historical approach.
Just as it is impossible to understand the religion of Torah
or the spiritual significance of Talmudic discussion in the
history of Jewry without a real attempt to enter sympatheti-
cally into the actual experience of those Jews who were led
by such paths both into the presence of God and into
successful and creative living, so also it is impossible really
to understand either the Gospels or the letters of Paul
unless we have tried to feel what their belief in Jesus as
Messiah meant to the early Christians. It is the central
phrase of Paul's gospel. It is the motive power of his life
and has nothing to do with the Law or with any matter of
controversy, but is comprehended in the two words, "in
Christ." They occur in almost every paragraph of his
letters, and convey not an intellectual conviction but an
overpowering personal experience.

Such a statement is not intended to deny the importance
of the freest and most searching criticism of the sources and
documents of either religion, so long as we realise that we
cannot get finality from such methods. We use them, knowing that our successors may add new knowledge and new
interpretations. But we use them also believing that it is the
will of God that we shall seek in this field, as in others, to
understand His purpose by the use of all the intellectual
insights and means of investigation with which He has
endowed us.

On the other hand, it is equally important to recognise
that the historical approach to an issue whose importance
is basically theological has certain rights. Treatment of a
subject which would be entirely legitimate in a sermon
or devotional commentary can often result in misrepresentation when it is made the basis of historical judgments.
This will apply particularly in the subject under consideration when the Gospels denounce those imperfections and
failures of Pharisaism which are, in fact, the imperfections
and failures of all institutional religions. Such denunciations
are not in themselves historical evidence to be used to
distinguish the Pharisees from other religious teachers.

It is as true of the Roman Catholic priest, the Protestant minister and the Jewish rabbi to-day as it was of the Pharisees of the first century, to say that some keep the keys of the Kingdom of Heaven and neither enter themselves nor permit others to enter, that they bury their talent in the ground and so on. These would only be appropriately considered in a historical study of this kind if it could be shown that such was either the intention of Pharisaism, or the inevitable product of Pharisaic developments, and neither statement would be historically true. Attempts have sometimes been made to say that such condemnations were particularly true of the Pharisaism of the generation of Jesus; but for this there is no historical evidence. Indeed, the fact that Pharisaism rallied so magnificiently forty years later from the shock of the war with Rome and the total destruction of the Temple and the whole religious ministry related to the Temple, is a strong argument that the Pharisaism of the days of Jesus was no worse than that of preceding or subsequent generations. It is in His relation to Pharisaism, and not to individual Pharisees, to the Law and not to individual laws, that the position of Jesus must be estimated.

Before this can be done, however, we must consider the nature of our sources. Just because we are dealing with shades of meaning and divergences of opinion, the reliability of the actual language in which they are reported becomes exceedingly important. From the Christian side we have the four accounts of the life of Jesus associated with the names of Mark, Luke, Matthew and John; but we have no equivalent Jewish sources. Moreover, the Gospels were not written in order to provide us with answers to the questions which to-day we naturally ask. They are all the product of various first-century conditions, and of the trends of thought and interest in different first-century churches. For we have to realise that the Gospels do not come first; they did not create the Church: it was the Church which created the Gospels as the first generation of Christians was passing away and the End delayed to come. Even the earliest of them, therefore, belongs to the generation after the

events which they narrate, though there must have been
eye-witnesses to those events still alive at the time when
they were first written. Moreover, they were written, not
primarily to draw in outsiders, or to explain to outsiders
the nature of the Christian faith, but to supplement, within
the Christian community, the oral teaching given by
Christian preachers. This is made very clear by the preface
to the Third Gospel:

> "Forasmuch as many have taken in hand to set forth in
> order a declaration of those things which are most surely
> believed among us, even as they delivered them unto us,
> which from the beginning were eyewitnesses and ministers
> of the word, it seemed good to me also, having had perfect
> understanding of all things from the very first, to write
> unto thee in order, most excellent Theophilus, that thou
> mightest know the certainty of those things wherein thou
> hast been instructed." [1]

The Gospels have thus none of the characteristics of the
Christian Apologetics addressed to the pagan world in the
second century, nor are they comparable to modern bio-
graphies. Their authors were not concerned to answer the
kind of questions which apologetic would naturally raise,
nor to give a comprehensive analysis of the character and
teaching of Jesus. They clearly reveal definite doctrinal
points of view, but they were intended to illustrate and
define these points of view to those who already accepted,
or were in process of accepting, the faith in Jesus as Lord
and Saviour, and not to prove them to opponents or outsiders. The Gospel of Matthew has a Jewish interest; but
it was not written for non-Christian Jews. The Gospel of
Luke is concerned to show the implications of universalism
in the life of Jesus; but it was written for Roman Christians,
not for Roman pagans. But even for Christians the Gospels
were not written to give a systematic picture of the teaching
of Jesus on all the different theological and ethical problems
involved in the Christian life. From whatever standpoint
we approach them, they are always elusive.

We must accept also that we are never likely to get absolute finality on any important question of their interpretation. One school of New Testament criticism succeeds another, though each leaves some new residue of knowledge and insight behind it. Each in its turn appears convincing on details; but all, in so far as they attempt to explain deeper issues by their single formulas, break down at some theological or historical point. In the first flush of the discovery of new techniques of literary analysis in the nineteenth century, scholars of the famous Tübingen school of Protestant theologians confidently declared the whole New Testament to be a document of the organised Church, not earlier than the second century. For them the figures of Jesus and, to some extent, Paul, were such shadowy abstractions that some members of this school came to the logical position of denying that they had ever actually lived. But such scholars only landed themselves in the deeper problem of explaining how, without Jesus, the Christian Church ever began or sustained its existence. To-day the extremists of the current interpretation, known as Form Criticism, have produced almost similar results from an entirely different method of analysis. They accept the existence of Jesus, but proclaim that we have no guarantee that we know any word or incident of His life. And the result is the equal absurdity of positing the authors of the Gospels and their written sources to have been a group of men of incredible brilliance who could build up a composite and imaginary picture of a person, who did actually exist, yet without any reference to his existence; which picture is astonishingly coherent in all the subtle intangibles in which such creative artists would be expected to differ, but breaks down on the simplest mutual confirmation as to the externals of biography.

Just as the attempt to deny the historical existence of Jesus has been abandoned, so also most modern scholars have rejected the idea that the Gospels themselves are literary compositions of a period so late that their historical significance is nil. But, if it be now accepted that they are documents

of the first century, it is important to realise that this
is the century of bitter controversy between the Synagogue
and the nascent Church, and that this controversy affects
particularly the subject of this enquiry—the mutual relations between Jesus and the Jewish leaders of his day. The
dates to which the Gospels are usually attributed—Mark,
c. 65, Luke, c. 75 or a few years later, Matthew between 85
and 95, and John around the turn of the century—would be
confirmed by the evidence they offer in this particular
field; and would explain why there is often a slight but consistent increase in anti-Jewish feeling as a single incident is
retold from source to source. The description of the teaching
of John the Baptist, and one of the miracles of healing, will
illustrate the point. While Mark does not specify what was
the actual proclamation of John the Baptist to different
groups of his hearers, Luke says of his general message:

"Then said he to the multitude that came forth to be
baptised of him, O generation of vipers, who warned you
to flee from the wrath to come? Bring forth therefore
fruits worthy of repentance, and begin not to say within
yourselves, We have Abraham to our father: for I say unto
you, that God is able of these stones to raise up children
unto Abraham."[2]

But Matthew, who gives even fuller details, gives this particular message only "when he saw many of the Pharisees
and Sadducees come to his baptism."[3]

The incident of healing is thus described by Mark:[4]

"And again he entered into Capernaum after some
days; and it was noised that he was in the house. And
straightway many were gathered together, insomuch that
there was no room to receive them, no, not so much as
about the door: and he preached the word unto them. And
they come unto him, bringing one sick of the palsy, which
was borne of four. And when they could not come nigh
unto him for the press, they uncovered the roof where he
was: and when they had broken it up, they let down the

bed wherein the sick of the palsy lay. When Jesus saw their faith he said unto the sick of the palsy, Son, thy sins be forgiven thee. But there were certain of the scribes sitting there, and reasoning in their hearts, Why does this man thus speak blasphemies? who can forgive sins but God only? And immediately when Jesus perceived in his spirit that they so reasoned within themselves, he said unto them, Why reason ye these things in your hearts? Whether is it easier to say to the sick of the palsy, Thy sins are forgiven thee: or to say, Arise, and take up thy bed, and walk? But that ye may know that the Son of man hath power on earth to forgive sins (he saith to the sick of the palsy) I say unto thee, Arise and take up thy bed, and go thy way into thine house. And immediately he arose, took up the bed, and went forth before them all; insomuch that they were all amazed, and glorified God, saying, We never saw it on this fashion."

In this account the surprise of the scribes is reasonably expressed; and the reply of Jesus is not hostile. Luke says: "Who is this which speaketh blasphemies?" which is certainly less friendly. The reply of Jesus is unaltered.[5] In Matthew the comment of the scribes to themselves is simply, "This man blasphemeth," and the reply of Jesus is: "Wherefore think ye evil in your hearts?"[6] At the end of the incident Mark and Luke say that "all" were filled with amazement and glorified God. Matthew says that it was the multitudes, not the leaders, who glorified God. They are small points, but they constantly occur. Their importance lies in the evidence they give as to the state of opinion at the precise time and place at which the three Gospels were written. That in general there was a steady increase of hostility, culminating in the separation of the two religions, we know from subsequent history; the interest of the first Gospel in the evidence from prophecy that Jesus was the Messiah comes to be the basis of a whole literature of apologetic and polemic towards Judaism; the interest of the third in emphasising the Gentiles who came into contact with Jesus likewise reflects a stage in the development of the Church's attitude to the Roman authorities, to the Gentile converts, and to the place of believing Gentile and un-believing Jew in their Messianic conceptions. But, once we realise this background and its influence on tone and choice of incident, we can accept the first three Gospels as belonging to a single consistent tradition. The real problem arises, from the discrepancies which exist, not between any of them, but between all of them and the fourth.

The Fourth Gospel, the Gospel according to John, stands apart in its whole treatment of the life and teaching of Jesus. If we were to accept it as evidence of the historical develop-ment of the situation between Jesus and Judaism, then we would need totally to revise our picture of events. For this Gospel implies that there was a profound enmity on the part of "the Jews" to His person and teaching from the very beginning; and that this was based on the public claim of Jesus to be Messiah and divine from the very outset of His ministry, a claim which, if not made absolutely openly, was at least made with such thinly veiled allusions that they were susceptible of no other, or lesser, explanation. That this is what actually happened I find it impossible to believe; but that does not mean that the Gospel contains no historical material. Actually, it is the only Gospel which contains a chronological framework, a chronology based on the Jewish feasts;[7] and though many scholars dismiss this framework as a literary device, yet there is no reason to doubt that its accounts of various visits to Jerusalem and Judæa before the final visit are based on a genuine tradi-tion. But when we come to our precise subject, the relations of Jesus to Jews and Judaism, we can only say with Dr. Temple[8] that the Gospel embodies the interpretative ex-pression of a memory and that the final relationship between the two parties is in memory hardened into antagonism from the outset. Thus the author refers to "the Jews" as though the words automatically excluded Jesus and the disciples;[9] and the Jewish feasts are mentioned as though Jesus visited them as an outsider. The other important point on which the author diverges from the synoptic picture is that he puts the priests and Pharisees in constant alliance against Jesus, and gives the Pharisees an equal share with the Temple authorities in the events leading to the Crucifixion.[10] All this can be taken to reflect, not only the ultimate breach between Jesus and the Jewish authorities which culminated in the Crucifixion, but equally the breach between the followers of Jesus and the successors to the Jewish authorities of His day which led to the separation of the two religions. In the environment of the author, the controversy was a thing of the past; and if the Gospel be dated about A.D. 100, that is itself historical evidence of the time at which the estrangement between the two religions, whose steps we trace in the synoptists, was complete in that environment.

Together with the accentuation of an anti-Jewish tone, another indication of the growing gulf between the two religions is the increasingly vague and inaccurate way in which differences of opinion within Jewry are treated, until in John "the Jews" are all put together as though Jesus and his Apostles were not Jewish.

While in terms of time we need to take into account the Johannine descriptions of visits to Jerusalem, in terms of the development of relations we have a more valuable source in Mark, whose sequence of events can be regarded as reliable from this standpoint. Luke changes it in order to bring out his particular interest in the universal significance of the life of Jesus. The most striking example of this is that he inserts at the very beginning of the public ministry of Jesus an event which Mark places much later.[11] Jesus preaches in his own town of Nazareth and the scene is thus described by Luke:[12]

"He came to Nazareth where he had been brought up; and, as his custom was, he went into the synagogue on the sabbath day, and stood up for to read. And there was delivered unto him the book of the prophet Esaias. And when he had opened the book, he found the place where it was written, The Spirit of the Lord is upon me, because he hath anointed me to preach the gospel to the poor; he hath sent me to heal the broken-hearted, to preach deliverance to the captives, and recovery of sight to the blind, to set at liberty them that are bruised, to preach the acceptable year of the Lord. And he closed the book, and he gave it again to the minister, and sat down. And the eyes of all them that were in the synagogue were fastened on him. And he began to say unto them, This day is this scripture fulfilled in your ears. And all bare him witness, and wondered at the gracious words which proceeded out of his mouth. And they said, Is not this Joseph's son? And he said unto them, Ye will surely say unto me this proverb, Physician, heal thyself: whatsoever we have heard done in Capernaum, do also here in thy country. And he said, Verily I say unto you, No prophet is accepted in his own country. But I tell you of a truth, many widows were in Israel in the days of Elias, when the heaven was shut up three years and six months, when a great famine was throughout all the land; But unto none of them was Elias sent, save unto Sarepta, a city of Sidon, unto a woman that was a widow. And many lepers were in Israel in the time of Eliseus the prophet; and none of them was cleansed, saving Naaman the Syrian. And all they in the synagogue, when they heard these things, were filled with wrath; And rose up, and thrust him out of the city, and led him unto the brow of the hill whereon their city was built, that they might cast him down headlong. But he passing through the midst of them went his way."

There is no evidence that in the early preaching of Jesus the most challenging statements aroused such hostility. It was after the quarrels with the Pharisees, and when His popularity began to wane, that men became less ready to listen to Him; and it is in this setting that Mark gives the story though he does not give the content of the sermon. Luke's purpose is to give at the very beginning the foretaste of what was to come, that the Gospel often rejected by Jews was readily accepted by Gentiles. Matthew is little concerned

with historical order at all. His arrangement is liturgical.[13]
It is designed to secure single blocks of teaching, and his narrative is little more than the frame for five such blocks. His
interest is to present his material so as to show Jesus as a new
interpreter of Torah (some would even say as the giver of a
new Torah) and the Sermon on the Mount balances the
revelation on Sinai. Hence he is much more inclined to con-
centrate attacks on the alternative interpreters of Torah,
i.e. the Pharisees and Pharisaic scribes, though he adds
nothing fundamentally to that which will be found in the
other sources.

It is this fact, that there are no fundamental differences in
the approaches of the three synoptists, that makes it possible to treat of the relations of Jesus with Judaism in a
single chapter. To give a detailed analysis of every one of the
incidents narrated by the different Gospels would need a
whole book, but here it is not necessary. For our purpose we
need only to select sufficient material to make His and their
attitude clear. Further, were there important contradictions
in the attitude of Jesus Himself on different occasions, or in
different accounts, it would be necessary to examine every
incident reported before we could obtain a due balance and
proportion for any conclusions suggested. But this also is
not the case; there is a naturalness and reasonableness in the
story as unfolded by Mark, which Matthew and Luke amplify
but do not contradict.

If, however, we are to rely on Mark for a historical narrative, we must still remember that biography, in the modern
sense, is only an incidental interest with him. His historical
facts are not adequate to give us a complete itinerary of the
public ministry of Jesus, or even to say how long it lasted.
All that we can assume is that the events which he records are
most likely to have happened in the order in which he
records them, and that they have not been rearranged to
suit some doctrinal or apologetic purpose, or merely lumped
together without historical intention, as the present school of
from criticism is apt to assert. For our purpose we need only
to consider the early history in Galilee and the final week in

Jerusalem. For all the elements in the disagreement between Jesus and the Pharisees are to be found in the former, and all the questions involved in the charge of "Jewish" responsibility for the Crucifixion in the latter. The picture which Mark paints of that early ministry is one of extraordinary freshness and charm.

Somewhere in the years between A.D. 25 and 30, there appeared in Galilee one of the itinerant preachers, familiar on the Jewish scene, whom men recognised as Jesus, son of a carpenter from Galilee. Like others of His kind, He wandered through the towns and villages preaching to the people, sometimes in the market place, sometimes on the open hills with their wide prospects of the lake and the distant hills of Samaria and Decapolis. His themes were illustrated from the objects of the countryside with which all His hearers were familiar, the gay flowers of spring, the cornfields and gardens, the ordinary daily life of craftsman and peasant, of merchant and housewife. On the Sabbaths He was often asked to speak in the synagogues, and there, as in the evenings in the market places, He quickly began to attract attention. Men were struck both by His personality and by His words, for "he taught them as one that had authority and not as the scribes."[14]. But this was not all. The new preacher began to display remarkable gifts of healing—gifts which always attract the wonder of the crowd, and which critics, faced with the miracles of modern psychiatry, are less disposed than their nineteenth-century predecessors to excise from the Gospel narratives as legendary accretions. Preaching one Sabbath in the synagogue in Capernaum—the predecessor of the Roman building whose ruins still rise beside the lake—Jesus was interrupted by one of the congregation. In the words of Mark—

"there was in their synagogue a man with an unclean spirit; and he cried out, saying, Let us alone; what have we to do with thee thou Jesus of Nazareth? Art thou come to destroy us? I know thee who thou art, the Holy One of God. And Jesus rebuked him, saying, Hold thy peace and come out of him. And when the unclean spirit had torn him, and cried out with a loud voice, he came out of him."[15]

It is not difficult to picture the astonishment which the incident created:

"and they were all amazed, insomuch that they questioned among themselves, saying, what thing is this? what new doctrine is this? for with authority commandeth he even the unclean spirits and they do obey him. And immediately his fame spread abroad throughout all the region round about Galilee."[16]

A band of followers attached themselves to His steps, both men and women; and as the crowds which He drew grew ever bigger and bigger, He began to attract the less desirable attention of the authorities, both religious and political. It was not at first that there was anything either unorthodox or seditious in His activities; but the times were dangerous for both religious and political life. Those who were concerned with the former could not but be conscious of the ring of Greek cities, on the sea coast and across the lake, from which pagan and immoral influences spread seductively into the centres of Jewish life; those whose concern was the latter had to watch carefully lest their few remaining liberties were taken away by the Roman authorities; and the need to watch was particularly urgent in Galilee, where Messianic speculation was in the air, and fierce taxation and harsh government had made the people restless and only too ready to rise in hopeless resistance if any spark was set to their smouldering discontent. For the Galileans were a fierce and intractable people. It was therefore with a special intensity that the activities of anyone who appeared out of the ordinary would be scrutinised.

In the early message of Jesus there was nothing to disturb either party. Though it centred in the idea of the Kingdom of Heaven, it contained neither the political appeals nor

the emotional denunciations which we associate with the
Messianic nationalism of the times or with later Christian
revivalism. It was clear teaching about men's relations
with God and with each other, and recalled men to the
realities of the spiritual life in a way which the religious
leaders could approve and the political ignore. But His
popularity, and the use which might be made of it by others,
must even at that time have appeared to the politicians
a potentially dangerous aspect of His activity.

Over how long a period this part of Mark's narrative
is spread we have no means of knowing; for Mark mentions
neither seasons nor festivals in it, though his order gives
a very logical sequence of events. Some time after the healing
of the "man with an unclean spirit" Jesus encountered a
leper, and His words to him show a most careful insistence
on the fulfilment of the law. "See," said Jesus, "thou say
nothing to any man: but go show thyself to the priest, and
offer for thy cleansing those things which Moses commanded,
for a testimony unto them."[17] About this there could be no
uneasiness; but then occurs the healing which has already
been described in which Jesus saw that part of the cure
was to assure the patient that his sins were forgiven, and a
further incident in which He willingly shared a meal with
publicans and sinners,[18] who were extremely unlikely
to have kept to the strict Pharisaic regulations about the
food they ate or the manner in which they ate it. Neither
was in itself enough to condemn Him; but they were
certainly not what was expected of an orthodox religious
teacher. But it is noticeable that in both cases He was ready
to give a reasonable interpretation of His action, an explanation which showed that He did not regard the criticism
as necessarily factious or hostile. In one case the fact of the
cure was used as a justification. In the other He replied
that He had "come not to call the righteous but sinners."
And we must remember that at that time the Pharisees,
even when they would consider that His actions did not
conform to their own standards, would have been slow to
condemn them outright as "un-Jewish." For the Judaism

of the period was a religion of many sects and practices.

Then, however, occurred two incidents connected with the Sabbath which touched them more vitally, for the scrupulous observance of the Sabbath lay at the very heart of their religious teaching. In the first case, Jesus allowed His disciples to pluck and rub grains of corn on the Sabbath, and in the second He healed a man in the synagogue who was in no danger of his life.[19] In each case the Pharisees vigorously criticised Him, and He as vigorously defended Himself. There is nothing to suggest that the issue was concerned with the actual observance or non-observance of the Sabbath. But the attitude of Jesus to its observance showed a willingness to ignore the fences about the Sabbath which Pharisaic Judaism had erected, and other stories which occur in all the Gospels reveal the accuracy of this feeling of the Pharisees. Doubtless the fact that He denounced the failings of Pharisaism angered His opponents, as have the denunciations of all reformers angered the established religious powers. But that is irrelevant to the main issue, the deep difference in religious attitude; for, though the matter may appear to be trifling, it concealed a profound difference of outlook. It is not necessary for our purpose to follow the narrative further; for this remains the heart of the issue.

It was concerned with the development of interpretation, and the methods adopted by the Pharisees to embody their interpretations in regulations of daily life (Halachah). It was not concerned with the recognition of Torah itself, nor even with the right of Pharisaism to develop new interpretations. We have plain statements of Jesus' respect for the Law, and even for the Pharisees; and with our present knowledge of the sources behind the Gospels we can see that the authenticity of these statements was part of the common tradition of the early Church, for they are to be found in all the sources, except for the special material in Luke which is not concerned with such questions. Thus Mark reports the question: "What shall I do that I may inherit eternal life?" and the answer of Jesus: "Thou knowest the commandments."[20] There is also His definition of the greatest commandments.[21] From the source common to Matthew and Luke, known as Q, both Gospels report the words: "ye pay tithe of mint, and anise and cummin and have omitted the weightier matters of the law, judgment, mercy, and faith: these ought ye to have done, and not to leave the other undone";[22] while Matthew from his special source reports the two strongest of these sayings:

> "Think not that I am come to destroy the law or the prophets: I am not come to destroy, but to fulfil. For verily I say unto you, Till heaven and earth pass, one jot or one tittle shall in no wise pass from the law, till all be fulfilled."

and:

> "The scribes and the Pharisees sit in Moses' seat: All therefore whatsoever they bid you observe, that observe and do."[23]

These statements seem quite unequivocal, and there is no ground for ascribing them to a later Christian tradition, since they were recorded at a time when Christian feeling was running in the opposite direction. To them must be added a very important fact which is too often ignored because it is not controversial. There is no evidence that his Pharisaic opponents criticised the teaching of Jesus on the subject of God, the Kingdom of Heaven, sin, prayer, repentance and forgiveness. On none of these subjects is there evidence that His teaching appeared "un-Jewish."

If this be the fact then we must ask ourselves why either side troubled to attack the other. All our sources agree that the Pharisees showed more hostility to Jesus at this stage of His ministry than any other Jewish group. Jesus likewise attacked the Pharisees in a way He attacked none of the other sects. Why? There appear to be two answers. In the first place, both Jesus and the Pharisees shared a deep concern for the spiritual life and happiness of ordinary people. The Pharisees were the democratic group in Jewry and in Judaism. Though they separated themselves from the non-observant by a series of ritual regulations which impeded close intercourse, yet they were not a closed order, and they desired ordinary people to do the same. It was ordinary people that they wished to draw into their fold by persuading them also to adopt the way of life they themselves followed and by separating themselves from the non-observant increase the number of faithful Israelites. The mission of Jesus was directed to exactly the same people. In the second place, each of the two opponents paid the other the compliment of considering them the most important alternative teachers to themselves. Jesus did not waste His time on things that did not matter. He concerned Himself with the Pharisees because in His view they were so nearly right. The Pharisees concerned themselves with Him because he was so obviously being successful in bringing a new reality of God and a new fellowship between men into the lives of ordinary people. In such a situation details rightly assume an importance they would not otherwise possess.

In limiting the controversy to the development of interpretation, we have a still further question to decide. If we accept that Jesus did not endorse current Pharisaic developments, we must still define what form that disagreement assumed. The sphere of disagreement was the sphere of the development of Halachah, i.e. regulations which had to be obeyed. Did, then, Jesus lay down alternative Halachah? The issue has this importance—that if He did, then He was founding a separate religion. For it did not lie with any layman to issue Halachah, and no one has suggested that Jesus, though He had obviously received the religious education of a loyal Jew, had been specially trained as a rabbi or scribe. It is significant that the Pharisees did not make this particular charge against Him. There is, however, one set of passages which, if they are fully authentic in their present form, have a definitely halachic character. These are the passages dealing with divorce. According to Luke, Jesus forbad divorce entirely;[24] according to Matthew, He allowed it only if the wife had committed adultery.[25] Here Jesus was certainly departing from the much easier Jewish procedure, but it still remains to be decided whether He was stating a desirable ideal or a halachic law which was to be enforced among his followers. Those Christian Churches which have founded their canon law upon these verses evidently hold the latter interpretation. But they overlook the curious situation that, if this is so, then Jesus, in deliberately founding a new religion, gave it only one absolute law—incidentally, the variations of text make it uncertain what this law is—that there was to be no divorce. This is surely an inadequate basis for a religion, and it is more reasonable to assume that the halachic form of the text is due to the writer of the Gospel, and that Jesus is following here His usual practice of reminding men of the perfection to which they are called as sons of God. And there is ample support in the text for this interpretation. It was not more or different Halachah that Jesus desired, but deeper spiritual insight. The peculiarities of the traditional Christian attitude to divorce are thrown into even greater relief by a consideration of the other issue on which it might be, and indeed is, argued that the teaching of Jesus has a halachic and obligatory character. This is the question of Christian participation in war, a subject on which the general Christian tradition has—rightly or wrongly—definitely rejected the halachic, i.e. pacifist, interpretation of the teaching of Jesus.

The conflict was not over two schools of Halachah. It was concerned with two methods of bringing men into contact with the living God. The method of Jesus has often been held by Christian scholars to be a return to the methods of the prophets. He was not concerned with generalisations, with abstractions or with ideals, but with a concrete perfection here and now. He called men to get directly to the heart of the question. His opening proclamation,[26] "Repent, for the kingdom of heaven is at hand," appears as a result of centuries of Christian interpretation to lay its main emphasis on the backward examination of our sins; and from the earliest days the Church has interpreted the second half in terms of time—the Kingdom is about to come. But, however universal these interpretations are, they are not compelled by the Greek, nor by the Aramaic which lies behind the Greek. The word Jesus may be assumed to have used for "repent" contains the central idea of "return" (it is the same root as the Hebrew title given to the Jews who have returned to Palestine—the Yishuv, the returning ones). It looks to a future objective related to a positive past knowledge, not to the negative sins of the past. The Greek word contains a similar idea—change your outlook (*metanoeite*). Similarly "at hand" could refer to space as much as to time. I believe that the message should be rendered "return to God and His Kingdom is all round you *now*" rather than "repent for your past sins because the judgment of God is about to come upon you." It is another way of stating, "seek ye first the Kingdom of God and His righteousness, and all these things shall be added unto you."[27]

All through His preaching there is the same direct call to get to the heart of things, and such an attitude naturally ignored the "fences" and "details" of Pharisaic Halachah, not because it opposed them, but because it scarcely noticed them. It often exaggerated details deliberately to make the central point clear, offering counsel which was not meant always to be literally carried out, as was the Halachah of the Pharisees. There are innumerable examples of this: "If thy right hand offend thee, cut it off"; "If any man will sue thee at the law and take away thy coat, let him have thy cloke also."[28] Such an attitude led naturally to a direct contradiction of Halachah, as in the controversies over the Sabbath. It is not the observance of the Sabbath itself which is at issue. *But* the Sabbath was made for man and not man for the Sabbath.[29] Man should not work, but it was only as the result of an elaborate and artificial definition that the two subjects of Sabbath controversy could be called "work." To rub ears of corn or to heal a sick man by a touch had only become unlawful as a result of the erection of Pharisaic fences.

The greatest tragedy in the subsequent relations of the two religions is that the Christian tradition has seen in this conflict a quarrel in which Jesus stood for fundamental principles, while the Pharisees cared only for formal and spiritually meaningless details. Such an attitude has only been possible because the Christian Church has been, and in large measure still is, profoundly ignorant of the nature of Pharisaic Judaism. The issue was not these precise definitions of Pharisaic Halachah, but the religious attitude which they were likely to create. They would tend to increase the importance of externals and of external conformity, and this has in fact been an ever-present danger in rabbinic Judaism. But the Christian tradition is wholly wrong in believing that Jesus held that the Pharisees were *only* concerned to inculcate such externals in place of spiritual relations between men and their Father in Heaven.

Pharisaism actually saw in the constant creation of regular habits an essential method of inculcating into the lives of the whole people the religion of the prophets. It was, in Christian terminology, an essentially sacramental religion, constantly insisting on an outward and visible sign to an inward and spiritual grace. But in the mind of Jesus His Pharisaic contemporaries had, in the performance of this task, come to lay such emphasis on the outward and visible sign that ordinary men were in very great danger of substituting conformity on details for inward and spiritual religion. The whole emphasis of the teaching of Jesus therefore lay in religious insight and sensitive spiritual intuition. Be conscious, He said, that God is your Father and men are your brothers, and you will fulfil the Law instinctively. This attitude is perfectly expressed in the words of Paul:[30]

"Owe no man anything but to love one another: for he that loveth another hath fulfilled the law. For this, thou shalt not commit adultery, thou shalt not kill, thou shalt not steal, thou shalt not bear false witness, thou shalt not covet; and if there be any other commandment, it is briefly comprehended in this saying, namely,

Thou shalt love thy neighbour as thyself. Love worketh no ill to his neighbour; therefore love is the fulfilling of the law."

If we say, as the evidence entitles us to, that the method of preaching adopted by Jesus was a return to that of the prophets, then it is important to remember that the task undertaken by the Pharisees and their predecessors was not to create a new religion, different from that of the prophets, but precisely to make prophetic religion a reality in daily life. For the prophets had signally failed to change the habits of their contemporaries. To take the most fundamental issue of all. In spite of their constant denunciations they never succeeded in stamping out idolatry among the people of Israel, as the experience of Jeremiah in the last days of the kingdom make clear.[31] But in the whole of the New Testament there is no single suggestion that actual worship by Jews of the gods of the heathen round about them was a problem for either Jesus or the Pharisees. And this result had been secured not by a continuance of the prophetic method, nor by the disappearance of rival gods in the territory inhabited by Jews, but by the introduction of the method of the Pharisees. The predecessors of the Pharisees did not merely "preserve Judaism"; they preserved *prophetic* Judaism by weaving it into the warp and woof of Jewish daily life—that is, by the creation of new habits. Now if, on the one hand, it was natural that such a method should at times overpass the limits of the sensible, and multiply regulations, where in fact such multiplication did not serve the ultimate end they had in view, on the other hand their work was by no means completed in the time of Jesus and its result securely attained. They could not therefore view with indifference a scucessful preacher, even if his objectives were the same, who both followed a method they believed by their experience to be unsuccessful, and actually made their task more difficult by encouraging people to think that they were themselves leading people away from and not towards the ideal of a life lived in contact with God.

From this standpoint, it is easy to see why they made a particularly vicious attack on the healing powers manifested by
Jesus, accusing Him of using the aid of the devil.[32] They
aroused far too much emotional enthusiasm, which would
not of itself lead to any reformation of life; and they gave a
glamorous setting to the healer which predisposed men
without due reflection to accept what He then said as a
teacher.

It is important to remember that both the protagonists
actually recognised the potential dangers of their own line
of action. Pharisees denounced insincere and hypocritical
Pharisees as vigorously as did Jesus;[33] and Jesus disapproved
of the crowds following Him just to see works of healing as
definitely as did the Pharisees.[34] But Jesus believed in
bringing men to God by developing an ever more sensitive
spiritual intuition; and the Pharisees believed in bringing
men to God by the continuous inculcation of habits which
would recall the presence and the reality of God in every
action of their daily lives. History has shown that by the
paths of both Jesus and the Pharisees men do in fact come
into the presence of God. It has shown likewise in each
religion a considerable element of the method of the other.
But the separation of the two religions and the profound
differences consequent on their subsequent development
show equally that they are two methods, and that men have
not yet found the way to bring them into a full creative
unity.

It may appear curious to have made no mention of the
Messianic claim of Jesus as a cause of conflict between Him
and the Pharisees. But belief in a Messiah was not an invention of the Christians; it was a wholly Jewish belief, which
Pharisees shared with all other Jews. They would have had
no ground for opposing a Jew simply on the basis that he
claimed to be Messiah. The issue would have been concerned
with the validation of his claim. In this case we can say that
the Pharisees, in view of their attitude to the teaching of
Jesus, would not have accepted His Messianic claims, *had He
made them openly, and made them also the basis of His authority to*

teach as He did. That Jesus did adopt such an attitude is clearly assumed by the author of the Gospel of John.[35] But the truth seems to be rather with the synoptists, that Jesus let His life and teaching speak for themselves and made no open claim to be the Messiah. He deprecated any reference to such claims being made on His behalf.[36] The Messianic issue is therefore properly concerned with the events consequent on the foundation of the Church and the development of Christology. It is something separate from the political use by the High Priest and his Council of a political charge of attempting to make Himself king of the Jews which formed the basis of His surrender to Pilate.

In the actual circumstances of the time, the Pharisees had far more power to undermine the teaching of Jesus than He had to destroy their influence with the people. They were not only more numerous, but they possessed in their religious courts considerable legal powers. There is no evidence in our sources that they used such powers during the ministry of Jesus. Even on the issue of His healings, where they might have brought a formal accusation of witchcraft, they appear to have confined themselves to verbal condemnations. On one occasion they are actually reported to have warned Jesus that the political authorities were planning to arrest Him.[37]

The central issue, however, is their attitude to His final arrest and condemnation in Jerusalem. To understand this part of the story, we must turn, first to the Herodians in Galilee, then to the "priests, elders and scribes" in Jerusalem. Two events of political significance are reported of the period of Jesus' ministry in Galilee. On one occasion the Pharisees and the "Herodians" are said to have determined to put Him to death.[38] In the event no action was taken, showing that neither the religious nor the political leaders had really made up their minds about Him. Jesus withdrew from the more populous centres, and spent part of His time outside the jurisdiction of Herod altogether. There is also a statement in the Fourth Gospel that on one occasion the Galilean crowd tried to make Him into a king.[39] Such an incident

CJC

is quite possible during the period of His popularity. The evidence for neither event can be called first-class. The synoptists know nothing of what was presumably a plot of the Zealots to make Jesus their tool, and no recorded teaching of Jesus would have caused Him to receive a death sentence in a Pharisaic court. But the general impression these two narratives leave, that it would have needed little more for either the political or religious leaders to decide to take action to stop His activities, may well be true. The real action, however, lies in the events of the last week in Jerusalem.

A great many problems connected with the arrest and trial would be solved if we accepted a suggestion recently made[40] that the Jewish court was not, as usually supposed, the religious Sanhedrin, but the political council of the High Priest. From rabbinical literature, and from historical narratives dealing with the period following the war with Rome, we are familiar with a "Sanhedrin" which was a formal religious court, composed of members of the Pharisaic party, presided over by a President who was not the High Priest, and possessing strict rules of procedure. At the time of Jesus this court appears to have possessed a poor reputation; and it is quite possible that the general reforms which followed the fall of Jerusalem led to a tightening up of its procedure; but we possess very little direct evidence as to what may have been possible at this exact time. Moreover, there is substantial evidence to show that, before the loss of political autonomy, there was another council, also called in Greek *sunedrion*, which was constituted at the will of the High Priest, and acted as his political court and adviser. The membership of this council consisted in the main of members of the High Priestly party, i.e. the Sadducees; though there is no reason to believe that it was more formally constituted than the Privy Council of a medieval king, to which it corresponded in function. Its membership might thus vary from time to time or on different occasions, and depend on the choice of the High Priest.

If we assume that the "priests, elders and scribes" before

whom first Jesus, and then later Peter and Paul, appeared[41] formed, in fact, the political council, then we can say that it was primarily a Sadducaic body. The description of its members as "priests, elders and scribes" is not synonymous with "priests, elders and Pharisees"; for there were scribes attached to both schools of interpretation, the Pharisaic and the Sadducaic. It would then be clear, on the one hand, that no Pharisees intervened on behalf of Jesus, as did Gamaliel on behalf of Peter, and other Pharisees on behalf of Paul; but, on the other, there would be no evidence that any Pharisees were present during the two hastily summoned meetings of the High Priest's councillors at which the political charge against Jesus was framed, and the decision taken to hand Him over to Rome on a capital charge. In the synoptic Gospels all references to the Pharisees cease after their questioning of Jesus at the beginning of Holy Week; and there is nothing improbable in the suggestion that the High Priest would not have summoned leaders of the Pharisaic party to assist in a piece of political rigging to which they might well have objected—as they did object to condemnations of the two Apostles on much less serious charges. This would be wholly consistent with what we know of Pharisaic conceptions of justice, as well as what we know of the procedure of the religious Sanhedrin. And one of our main difficulties is that the sequence of events described in the Gospels seriously disagreed with this procedure.

It is clear in all the Gospel accounts that the council which was concerned with the arrest of Jesus was presided over by the High Priest. This was true of the political council, but not of the religious. If we assume that it was therefore with the political council that we have to do, then the difficulties disappear that the whole procedure of arrest and trial at night and other details were illegal according to what we know of the religious council. The political council could naturally fit its procedure to the emergencies of political life. A second difficulty which is removed by this solution is that there is no evidence that the religious council was unable to carry out its own decisions, including the death sentence, for religious offences in which the Romans would have had no interest; whereas there is evidence, and it conforms also to the general political situation, that the Romans would be concerned with political offences of sufficient gravity to merit death, and that the political council could not inflict it on its own responsibility.

One other point needs mention. There are still Christians who would hold the foregoing argument irrelevant in view of the cry of the crowds before Pilate: "his blood be on us and on our children."[42] This incident is peculiar to Matthew. It is part of the story of Pilate washing his hands to signify his innocence, whose authenticity is very doubtful. But even were it true, it would still be amazing that such Christians do not hold it to be cancelled by the appeal of Jesus himself from the Cross: "Father, forgive them; for they know not what they do."[43]

We can then assume that there is substantial probability that the sequence of events was as follows: the entry of Jesus into Jerusalem in a fashion which suggested a Messianic claim[44]—that is, riding on an ass and accompanied by crowds crying, "Hosanna to the Son of David"—aroused the alarm of the Temple authorities. Even though the discovery by the crowds that Jesus had no intention of leading a political revolt was followed by an immediate loss of popularity, yet He was evidently too dangerous a person to leave at liberty. The normal procedure was for such persons to be arrested by the Jewish authorities (with the aid, if needed, of Roman soldiers), examined in order to frame a clear charge for the Roman Governor, and then handed over to the Romans for actual trial and sentence. This is the procedure followed in the case of Jesus. He was arrested at night, examined (whether once or twice is uncertain) by the High Priest and his associates; the political charge of attempting to make Himself king was considered satisfactorily proved; and He was handed over to Pilate in the morning for judgment. A Roman scourging and execution followed.

It is probable that the many uncertainties concerned with details of the trial of Jesus will never be completely elucidated. There is, for example, the interesting fact that in the few references to His death in the Talmud there is no mention of a Roman condemnation and sentence. The entire action is assumed to be Jewish and, of course, justifiable. The references[45] are rare and show a good deal of confusion. But the charge is purely religious and not political. In various ways He was "a deceiver of the people." Modern Jewish apologetic has often sought to exculpate the Jews, or even to deny all Jewish responsibility, on the grounds that crucifixion is a Roman penalty. This, however, is not the issue. The Christian tradition has never denied that Jesus was executed by the Romans. The question is not that, but rather by what means did He come into the hands of the Romans on a capital charge? And here the answer must be that it was through some Jewish action, and the important issue is whether it was through the action of the religious or of the political authorities. The Christian tradition has always assumed that it was the former, and has ignored the evidence of the synoptists to which reference has already been made. It has held that in the Crucifixion it was not some Jews, but Judaism, which stands eternally condemned. With the further question of the rejection of Christian preaching by the majority of the Jewish people we shall deal in the next chapter. But here it can be said that, tragic as was the split between Jesus and the religious leaders of His day, the evidence is not such as to warrant this whole-hearted condemnation. Nor, in spite of the traditional assumptions, does Christian theology necessarily demand it. The Christian will naturally believe that in the controversies with the Pharisees Jesus was right. But the implication that this means that the Pharisees were wholly wrong, and preternaturally blind, easy though it is to make, is not a necessary consequence of this belief. It was a conflict between two rights, and it is in such conflicts that the essence of real tragedy resides.

To summarise the argument, we find a conflict between Jesus and the Pharisees, not based on the "un-Jewishness" of the teaching of Jesus, but on its rejection of contemporary

developments in Pharisaic interpretation. This conflict
was followed by a complete breach, but not, so far as the
evidence goes, by Pharisaic participation in a capital charge.
We find, however, a suspicion on the part of the political
officials, both in Galilee and Judæa, that here was a movement likely to lead to dangerous political consequences
for the nation. The behaviour of Jesus on His last visit
to Jerusalem confirmed the danger in their minds, and they
proceeded rapidly and efficiently to put Him in the hands
of Rome on a capital charge.

The Crucifixion ended whatever element of political
nationalism there was among the followers of Jesus. After
the refusal of Jesus to answer the question, "Wilt thou at
this time restore again the kingdom to Israel?"[46] we hear
no more of any political interest among His followers.
Instead, they turned to apocalyptic for an explanation of
the death of their Master, and reassured themselves with
the hope of His speedy return as supernatural judge and
ruler. The centre of their message was His resurrection,
and it is not until two or three decades later that, under the
influence of Paul, the emphasis moves from the resurrection
and return of Jesus to man's redemption through His death.

But once this development has taken place, Christian
theology moves into the lines which it has subsequently
followed. The Cross occupies the centre of the picture, and
still occupies it. Christianity becomes a religion which,
without the Cross, is as emptied of its kernel as Judaism
without Torah.

CHAPTER THREE

PAUL AND THE FOUNDATION OF THE CHRISTIAN CHURCH

THE EMERGENCE OF A Christian Church independent of its parent, the Jewish Synagogue, was a gradual process lasting between fifty and a hundred years. This is a long period for such events. The breaks of the Reformation were completed in the lifetimes of the Reformers, Luther, Calvin and others. But before the reforms which followed the war with Rome, Judaism possessed a wide tolerance of variety both of belief and practice, and it is in this fact that the reason lies why the passage to definitive schism was so long. The traditional assumption that the work of Paul was intended to lead to a break rests, partly at least, on a picture of the Judaism of his time, which takes inadequate account of the variety of Jewish beliefs now known to us from the study of the mass of apocalyptic literature preserved largely by the Eastern Churches. Important elements in Pauline teaching about the Messiah, which have been traditionally assigned either to his Hellenistic background or to his own original teaching, are now known to have close parallels in the writings of the apocalyptists. And though we can never be certain how much the texts have been modified or added to in the course of Christian transcription, yet we can safely deny that Paul's Messiah was as novel or as un-Jewish as he is usually assumed to be.

Many stages of the conflict between what were to become the two faiths must remain a matter of speculation, for adequate contemporary sources fail us from both sides; but in the Acts of the Apostles we are fortunate in having the work of one of the ablest ancient historians for our knowledge of the period immediately following the death of Jesus. His reliability has, of course, been constantly questioned by modern scholars. But from the point of view

of our particular interest in Jewish-Christian relations his
work stands up remarkably well to all criticism. A good test
of the accuracy of any historian of contemporary, or more
or less contemporary, events is whether, centuries later
and under totally different conditions, he still provides
answers to questions which he certainly never consciously
asked himself, but in which later ages have become
interested. From this test Luke—if as seems most likely,
he is the author in question—emerges triumphantly.
Either he used the records of the different churches (if such
existed at so early a period) with considerable care; or he
took great pains to search the memories of eyewitnesses and
hearers of the earliest preaching. While his sermons may
be "set pieces" in their phraseology, it is remarkable that
he provides in them evidence of the change which took
place in the attitude of early believers to the death of Jesus,
and does not project back to the earliest days the type of
sermon which would have been natural at the time at which
he wrote. In either case he gives us information as to the
nature of the pre-Pauline Gospel. The whole emphasis
was on the Resurrection of Jesus. Christianity was not yet
the religion of the Cross, and when it is referred to there is a
note of apology in the reference.[1] On the relations of the
new community with the Jewish authorities, and on the
gradual and almost accidental way in which the issue of the
admission of the Gentiles came to the fore, his evidence gives
a similar impression of reliability.

The disciples of Jesus, and those who joined themselves
to them in the first days, continued after the disappearance
of their Master to be full members of the Jewish community
of Jerusalem. Some were Pharisaic in their Judaism, some
were *amme ha-aretz* (the common folk). Some were of
Palestinian origin, some were recruited from the Hellenistic
synagogues. The only point which distinguished them from
their Jewish brethren was that they believed that they knew
the name of the coming Messiah and Judge. He was the
risen Jesus of Nazareth, who had passed through a life of
humiliation culminating in death, as a preliminary to

a glorious and triumphant return. This they expected in the immediate future. Holding this Messianic doctrine, the early Nazarenes (as they came to be called by other Jews) may be counted among the many groups who were expecting a miraculous and apocalyptic end to the Roman domination of Palestine; and it is not surprising if in the eyes of the authorities they should have been confused with those political nationalists who expected the same event, but believed it should be prepared and assisted by political rebellion. While it is true that there were undoubtedly individuals of this kind among the early followers of Jesus, and one of the faithful twelve is called Simon the Zealot, there is no evidence to show that there was any division of opinion on the eschatological issue in the early Church, or any party which believed that the Times of the End should be hastened by violent human action. We hear no more of the issue after the post-Resurrection question and answer reported in Acts:[2]

"When they therefore were come together, they asked of him, saying, Lord, wilt thou at this time restore again the kingdom to Israel? And he said unto them, It is not for you to know the times or the seasons, which the Father hath put in his own power."

From the beginning Peter assumed the leadership of the little band, and by his courageous preaching rapidly increased the numbers of the infant Church. The members practised communal living, not from economic motives, but because they believed the End of the Age to be near. The healing by Peter of a lame man in the full publicity of the Temple Courts[3] brought the existence of a sect devoted to the memory of the crucified Jesus to the attention of the priests; and Luke reminds us that the priests were Sadducees who would, therefore, be particularly out of sympathy with the preaching of the Resurrection which formed the core of the Apostles' message. Peter and John were arrested and brought before the High Priests.[4] Their boldness surprised their judges, but they found nothing on

which they could take action. They were given a warning
to stop their preaching and discharged. The Apostles paid
no attention to this warning; and their popularity increased,
and Peter's reputation as a healer of the sick grew in Jerusalem and the surrounding villages. [5] The Sadducean priests
again arrested them, but by some means they escaped
from prison and the following morning boldly returned to
the Temple. [6] This time they were scourged and released
with a further warning, the most interesting part of the
proceedings being the speech in their defence made by
Gamaliel: [7] "And now I say unto you, Refrain from these
men, and let them alone: for if this counsel or this work
be of men, it will come to nought: But if it be of God, ye
cannot overthrow it; lest haply ye be found even to fight
against God."

There is no reason to doubt the substantial accuracy of
this account of the earliest days of the Church. Nothing in it
is improbable. But the period of comparative immunity
was soon to come to an end. It was among the Hellenistic
Jews living in Jerusalem that the peace was first seriously
broken. Moved by the preaching and arguments of Stephen,
one of the Hellenistic leaders of the sect, the crowd seized
the preacher and hauled him before the authorities on the
charge that he had said that "this Jesus of Nazareth shall
destroy this place, and shall change the customs which
Moses delivered us." [8] That this conclusion would be drawn
from the preaching of Jesus was to be expected. The conflict between Jesus and the Pharisees was a real conflict, and
it was bound to be first reflected, and then exaggerated, by
His followers. Stephen was either executed or lynched by
the crowd of his accusers—the latter is the more probable
interpretation of the story—and the authorities decided that
the time had come for severe measures to be taken. Many
fled from Jerusalem, and a young Cilician Jew, Saul of
Tarsus, became the very active agent for hunting them out
in their refuges. [9] But the attempt at suppression failed.
In the first place, the spread of the members of the sect
to places they had not previously visited led to new

conversions. In the second place the issue became still more complicated by the fact that, in their dispersion, they began to come into contact with Gentiles, and that Gentiles were unquestionably attracted by their message. And in the third place, the authorities suffered the disastrous humiliation that their chief agent himself became a convert to the sect, while proceeding to Damascus with authority to root it out in that city.

That agent was the young Saul of Tarsus. He had been some time in Jerusalem studying under the great rabbi, Gamaliel.[10] As an enthusiastic adherent of Pharisaism, with a Diaspora background, he had been an early opponent of the spread of the Nazarene heresy among the Diaspora Jews in Jerusalem. Possibly because Damascus was a centre of various nationalistic Messianic groups, Saul was convinced that it was the danger spot in the spread of the new Nazarene movement, and therefore the place where it could be most effectively destroyed.[11] To do so he secured from the authorities a commission to proceed to Damascus armed with the full disciplinary measures permitted to the Jews by the Romans in their internal religious affairs.

Instead, he was converted to it. Such psychological revolutions have happened before, and will happen again, in passionate and religious temperaments. He had first come to Jerusalem, we may assume, because he was unsatisfied with the Judaism of his community in Tarsus. Possibly his spiritual quest had been only partially satisfied by the teaching of Gamaliel.[12] It is those uncertain of their own foundations who are often the most fervent advocates; they seek to silence their doubts by vehement action. That also is a phenomenon not unknown to religious history. The journey to Damascus would take several days. On the road he had time for his doubts and uncertainties to rise up against him. It culminated in a dramatic vision, and his loyalty was transferred, once and for all, to the sect he had persecuted, the Messiah he had denied. With this new convert, who changed his name from Saul to Paul, the new sect took on a different colour. Paul was no ignorant Galilean peasant. It is a reasonable assumption from his possession of Roman citizenship that his family was one of wealth and substance, for the number of Roman citizens to be found among the Jewish communities of provincial cities at this period must have been very small. He himself was rabbinically trained, and possessed of an exceptionally acute mind and an exceptionally deep spiritual insight. And he entered the sect at a critical moment in its development.

It is important to recognise that in dealing with any such group as the infant Church, we must not look for careful planning or for consistency. These are qualities we do not find in the early years of any such spiritual revival. When the Nazarenes scattered from Jerusalem, we need not therefore assume that either preaching to Samaritans and "God-fearing" Gentiles was carefully planned, or that the implication of the first acceptance of a Gentile (the Centurion Cornelius of Cæsarea whose conversion is described in Acts x) was fully recognised. The movement was still carried by the enthusiasm of its origin. Even the more "orthodox" Jews in the Jerusalem church were easily satisfied that[13] "God also to the Gentiles hath granted repentance unto life," when Peter told them of his experiences with Cornelius.

Of course, we do not know all the places in which Christian groups came into existence at this period—we do not, for example, hear of the founding of such a group at Damascus—but Luke tells us that the furthest point reached by those who had fled in the persecution following the condemnation of Stephen was the Syrian Antioch. It was there that the sect was first given the name "Christian" and that a systematic mission was first undertaken among actual Gentiles. Having heard of this mission, the Jerusalem church sent Joseph Barnabas on a visit of enquiry. What Barnabas saw convinced him of the rightness of the new move, and he set out to devise means of extending it.[14] Some years previously, when Paul had first visited Jerusalem after his dramatic conversion, and had been, not unnaturally, received with some suspicion by the older Christians, Barnabas had befriended him and stood sponsor for his sincerity.[15] Now his thoughts turned to this man as the right ally in the new venture, and he called Paul from his home in Tarsus. They spent a successful year together, touring as far as the Pisidian Antioch, and then both returned to Jerusalem to give a report of their work. This report was accepted, and the new policy was endorsed by the Church. An agreement was come to that Peter was to preach to the "circumcision" and Paul to the "uncircumcision."[16] But this was not so easily accepted by the stricter Judeo-Christians. First they demanded a separation in religious worship (especially the common meal) between Jewish and Gentile Christians; then they demanded that the Gentile Christians be made full Jews by circumcision and observance of the ceremonial as well as the moral law.[17] It is to be noted that the question is not whether Gentiles should be accepted, but only: on what basis are they to be admitted? It is sometimes argued that the admission of the Gentiles was the consequence of the brilliant strategy—or perverted ambition—of Paul. This is quite wrong. In the first place, the original steps were taken before Paul was in a position to influence Christian policy. But, in the second, the step itself contained nothing which was repellent to the Jewish conscience, once it is realised that the early Christians believed themselves to be living at the beginning of the Messianic Age. It was a belief shared by all Jews that the coming of the Messiah would institute a new relationship with the Gentile world.[18] But there was no authoritative definition of the form this relationship would take, and views ranged from the most political conquest to the most spiritual assimilation.

Among the early Christians there was likewise a division of opinion on this issue, and a council was called at Jerusalem to decide the matter. Paul and Barnabas, fresh from their practical experience in the Gentile world, argued for the most generous terms; some of the Jerusalem Church desired strict conformity with the ceremonial as well as the moral law. In the result there was no split, because the leader of the stricter group, James, accepted the views of Paul and Barnabas; and James was a Pharisee whose orthodoxy was approved even by Jews who did not accept his Messianic beliefs. The Council adopted the liberal Jewish view that the Noachic Commandments should be taught to Gentile converts, but not the ceremonial law.[19] This decision carried the approval of the bulk at least of the Jerusalem Christians and the Judeo-Christian Church, and there is no evidence that they ever went back on their acceptance. There was, however, a minority which objected, and which engaged in strenuous and continual opposition to Paul throughout his ministry. It is these who in Paul's letters are called the "Judaisers," and they were the recipients of the Apostle's most violent sarcasm and invective.[20] For they were indirectly attempting to undermine the whole of the teaching which he was giving, and had nothing effective of their own to substitute for it.

As with the early Church in general, so in particular with Paul, we shall not get at the truth if we look for consistency and careful planning in his words and work. We can only understand Paul as one of those God-possessed souls whose whole heart and mind is concentrated on a single objective. He was not a systematic theologian in the later Christian sense of the word, and he was often a very unclear controversialist. But when we find contradictions, the last motive to which we can ascribe them is to a cold and calculated insincerity, or even to a carefully thought-out diplomacy. But to say that Paul was not clear does not mean that he was superficial. He would be much easier to understand if he was. He is one of the greatest mystics of his age, but it is in the terms of his age that we need to approach him.

In order to form an estimate of the teaching of Paul, we have to consider the two sources in which that teaching is made known to us—his own letters and the Acts of the Apostles. The reconciliation of these two sources is often difficult; for if it is evident that we must accept his own letters as of primary importance, yet they themselves are capable of different interpretations depending on the weight which we give to the Acts of the Apostles. The point at issue is not Paul's Messianic doctrine, but his relations with Judaism after his "conversion." If we follow his letters exclusively—and this is what the Christian tradition has so far done—then we would assume that on his conversion Paul turned his back on the Pharisaic Judaism of his youth and on the Law which he then accepted, and that it is correct to say that from having been a "Jew" he became a "Christian." This, however, is not the picture which is given us by the Acts of the Apostles. Christian writers have too often over-emphasised the significance of two incidents which happened at the Pisidian Antioch and at Corinth.[21] On each occasion Paul's preaching stirred up a great controversy in the synagogue, and Paul, enraged at the opposition, announced vehemently: "It was necessary that the word of God should first have been spoken to you: but seeing ye put it from you, and judge yourselves unworthy of everlasting life, lo, we turn to the Gentiles." But these writers ignore that in each case Paul's first action in the next city which he visited—Iconium and Ephesus—was to seek out the Jewish community and preach in the synagogue.[22] These two incidents are much too slight a foundation on which to build a theory of a definite break between Paul and the Synagogue, or a definite abandonment by Paul of his Judaism.

Much more important is the sequence of events connected with Paul's last visit to Jerusalem, his arrest and his various speeches in his defence, both to Jews and Romans, for which Acts is the only source. They definitely raise the issue, not whether Paul's views created violent controversies—of that there is no doubt—but whether in his own mind Paul considered that by the beliefs which he had adopted he had ceased to be a loyal Pharisaic Jew, and had become something different, a "Christian." It is therefore important to consider whether we can use Acts as a reliable source, and, if so, to give these events in some detail. No book of the New Testament presents problems which are more insoluble along the normal lines of modern criticism than the Acts of the Apostles. It is agreed that it is by the same author as the Third Gospel; it contains three substantial

passages (xvi. 1–18, xx. 5–xxi. 25 (or to xxii. 24), xxvii.
1–xxviii. 16) in which the author uses "we," and it is generally
agreed that these are, or are directly built on, a diary
written by a travelling companion of Paul. But here agreement stops, and unfortunately for our purpose, which is
concerned with Paul's defence, the second "we" narrative
may only go as far as Paul's first interviews in Jerusalem
with the leaders of the Christian community, and in any
case stops at his arrest; and thereafter the "we" narrative is
not resumed until Paul's final departure from Palestine for
Rome. The question then is, whether the author is to be
relied on for the authenticity of the all-important intervening
narrative giving summaries of Paul's speeches in his defence
to various authorities.

In these various defences it is evident that the author
represents the Jews as violently hostile to Paul, and the
Romans (and the Romanised Jewish King Agrippa) as
seeing no basis for any charge against him. This is considered
by some scholars to indicate an "anti-Jewish" and "pro-
Roman" bias. But this would really only be so if it were
inherently improbable that the Jews should have been
hostile and the Romans indifferent; and there is no adequate
ground for either supposition, whether during these events
or earlier during Paul's missionary journeys. It is what
one would reasonably expect. It has also been suggested—
and for this there is some evidence—that the theological
suppositions of the author and of Paul differ, that Paul's
"theology" was more advanced than that of the author.
This we can accept without invalidating the accounts;
for there is no reason why the author, if a simpler and less
intellectual individual, should not have missed some of the
finer points of Paul's evolving theology without being either
inaccurate, biased or wholly imaginative in what he did
write.

The essential point of Paul's relation to Judaism
we must leave until the events have been recounted. At
the same time, there is no proof that the author *is* right
about the Jews and Romans; possibly the Romans were

more hostile than his evidence suggests; there is no proof that the author's modification of Paul's views may not have been due to deliberate bias; and a case can be built up to show Acts as a deliberately apologetic work presenting and omitting facts to fit a preconceived design. Acts, for example, tells us nothing of the conflict in the Corinthian Church which fills Paul's letters to the Corinthians, and this might indicate a deliberate desire to present a picture of a united community with only outside enemies. But again it is not conclusive. We are left with a choice, and we must make that choice, not on narrow or textual grounds, but on our general picture of the period within which the events are fitted. I have already suggested that I believe Acts to present an accurate picture of the first days of the new community, and the almost casual way in which the issue of Gentile admissions arose. My own choice is equally for the substantial accuracy of these closing chapters. The events were nearer the time of the narrator than the first days of the Church; once we recognise that Paul belongs to the period which preceded the separation of the two religions, and was not the conscious founder of a new Gentile Church, we must expect a less clear and defined relation to Judaism and the Jewish people than that traditionally held; and in this setting the chapters of Acts fit with reasonable appropriateness. We can, therefore, proceed to give the events in detail on the basis that, while the complete authenticity of Acts is unprovable, none of the arguments against it has yet proved sufficiently convincing to win any general acceptance.

From the moment when he planned his final visit to Jerusalem, Paul had no doubt that he would be running into danger. He was aware of the hostility which he had caused and expected to meet a difficult test of his loyalty to his Messiah in the witness which he felt called upon to give.[23] When he finally reached Jerusalem safely, he was warmly greeted by James, the head of the Judeo-Christian church, and by other Christian leaders in the city.[24] But they warned him of the controversy which existed about his teaching, and the opposition to it of many of the Christian Jews. As the report was that he was teaching *Jews* "to forsake Moses, saying that they ought not to circumcise their children, neither to walk after the customs,"[25] they felt that the best demonstration of the falsity of the charge would be that Paul should forthwith show his own loyalty to Judaism by both taking a Nazarite vow himself for seven days, and by accepting financial responsibility for four other Christians who had taken the same. This Paul willingly did.[26] It was towards the end of the seven days that some Jews from Asia recognised him in the Temple and called out to the crowds to seize him as the man who had taught "all men everywhere against the people, and the law and this place."[27] Rescued from the mob by the Roman guard, Paul obtained permission from the centurion to address the crowd. Speaking to them in Hebrew, he began an account of his life:[28]

> "I am verily a man which am a Jew, born in Tarsus, a city in Cilicia, yet brought up in this city at the feet of Gamaliel, and taught according to the perfect manner of the law of the fathers, and was zealous towards God, as ye all are this day."

When he began to describe his call to preach to the Gentiles a storm of opposition broke out and he was unable to ontinue. The centurion took him into the castle, and brought him before his commanding officer, who learned that Paul was a Roman citizen. The following day the officer requested the Temple authorities to state their charge against him, and Paul was brought before what we can assume to have been a political council, since it was presided over by the High Priest.[29] Acts does not relate what actual charge was made, for, as when Peter was tried, the issue turned on the resurrection and not on the Law. Paul insisted: "I am a Pharisee, the son of a Pharisee: of the hope and resurrection of the dead I am called in question,"[30] and the Pharisees, in order to oppose the Sadducees, protested that: "We find no evil in this man: but if a spirit or an angel hath spoken to him, let us not fight against God." [31] The meeting ended in some disorder, and Paul, withdrawn again by the Romans, was sent to the seat of the Roman Government at Cæsarea.

The next hearing was before Felix, the Roman Governor, and the accusation which was brought by the Temple authorities was that—

"we have found this man a pestilent fellow, and mover of sedition among all the Jews throughout the world, and a ringleader of the sect of the Nazarenes: who also hath gone about to profane the Temple: whom we took, and would have judged according to our law." [32]

Paul replied that "after the way which they call heresy, so worship I the God of my fathers, believing all things which are written in the law and in the prophets." [33] Again there was no decision, and Paul remained under arrest at Cæsarea for two years, until Felix was succeeded by Festus. To Festus Paul boldly asserted that "Neither against the law of the Jews, neither against the Temple, nor yet against Cæsar, have I offended any thing at all." [34] Festus then asked the Jewish King Agrippa to help him to clear up the charge against Paul, since he found it difficult to see what the issue really was. [35] Paul then made a long speech before Festus and Agrippa, describing his life and conversion, and beginning with the assertion that—

"My manner of life from my youth, which was at the first among mine own nation at Jerusalem, know all the Jews; which knew me from the beginning, if they would testify, that after the most straightest sect of our religion I lived a Pharisee. And now I stand and am judged for the hope of the promise made of God unto our fathers: Unto which promise our twelve tribes, instantly serving God day and night, hope to come." [36]

In the opinion of Agrippa the only thing which prevented Paul's release was the unfortunate fact that he had appealed to Cæsar, and must therefore be sent to the Imperial judgment seat.[37] Finally, when he had reached Rome, under guard, Paul called together the leaders of the Roman Jewish community and said to them that he had "committed nothing against the people, or customs of our fathers."[38]

Whoever was responsible for the whole of this series of events makes it clear that, in his mind, the original charge against Paul was false. Had Paul really abandoned the Law, he would not have been received with a warm welcome by the Jewish Christian leaders in Jerusalem. But James supported him in full knowledge of the nature of his teaching, though it is difficult for us to realise that it is very unlikely that he had ever seen any of Paul's letters. Had the Pharisaic members of the Council been aware that Paul was widely teaching Jews to abandon the Law, they would not have been deflected to his support by the fact that he also believed in the Resurrection. The charge which was brought by the Chief Priests to Cæsarea was a political one, having nothing to do with observance of the Law. Finally, Paul himself, in a series of utterances over three years, consistently maintained his continued loyalty to the Law of his fathers.

There is, then, no question but that the author of Acts represents Paul as having in no way quitted the faith of his fathers. There is no bold proclamation of a change from Judaism to Christianity such as we might expect. From the early days of the Church, theologians have recognised the difficulty of reconciling this with the language he uses in his letters. In various ways the traditional interpreters assume that Paul said less than he believed, or that he based his defence on expediency rather than principle. Two modern examples will illustrate what can still be said along these lines. Professor Menzies, in *Peake's Commentary* says of Paul's examination before the Chief Priest that "Paul played the *enfant terrible* among those grave and reverend elders,"[39] while Professor Rackham, in the *Westminster Commentary*, justifies his line of defence, while admitting it represents less than Paul's beliefs, by saying that it was suitable to the occasion.[40] But both really accord ill with the psychology of the Apostle, and it is preferable to choose between two alternatives: either Paul did not say what the author has attributed to him at all, and the whole narrative is a literary composition, or he said what he said because he meant it and believed it. Accepting the general reliability of Acts, I prefer the latter alternative. But this means that we shall not have rightly understood the meaning of the letters until we have found an interpretation consistent with Paul's own belief that he was throughout a loyal and observant Jew, interpreting his Judaism, as illuminated by his acceptance of the Jewish Messiah, to the Gentile world within which his life-work was to be spent.

The irony of the whole situation is that historical developments showed that the rioters were right about the effects of Paul's preaching. The Roman and Jewish authorities substituted political charges which they could not substantiate and Paul himself mistakenly assumed that others would interpret his intentions as he did himself. But within a couple of generations his teaching had led to the results the rioters foresaw—the abandonment by the Christian Churches which Paul had founded of the Judaism to which he sincerely believed himself to have remained loyal. But if they were right in asserting that Paul had succeeded in conveying the impression to his hearers—or some of them—that his message was concerned with the abolition of the Law, it is evident from the lines of Paul's successive speeches in his defence that in his own mind the things which he had said about the Law which could have implied its abolition were wholly secondary matters. Beyond brief but clear asseverations of his Jewish integrity, he paid no further attention to the charge, and in his defence passed to impassioned declarations of loyalty to his risen Messiah. This is the kernel of Paul's missionary enterprise, to bring to others the joy and peace and power that he himself had experienced in Christ. This issue between Paul and his accusers is continued into modern times by the conflicting attitudes of Jewish and Christian scholars towards him. There is no subject so difficult to treat from the standpoint of both the Jewish and the

Christian approach as is the place of Paul; with the inevitable consequence that in the following pages much of the argument will seem to either side unnecessary because they are unfamiliar with the method of approach or presuppositions of the other.

One point of this kind has already been mentioned: the assumption generally accepted in Jewish works that it was Paul who set out to make Christianity a Gentile religion, and that he therefore radically altered the religious development which might have flowed from the teaching of Jesus. Such a theory breaks down at the twin facts that the entry of Gentiles into the Church arose from Jewish conceptions of the Messianic age, and that it preceded the appearance of Paul on the scene. There is a comparable argument frequently used by Christian writers which is equally untenable. It is that Paul had to break with Judaism because the ethnic intolerance of the Jewish religion of his age was inseparable from it and was an absolute barrier to the fulfilment of the divine purpose in Sinai and Calvary; so that Paul, in his breakaway, was not only fulfilling the purpose of the Incarnation, but was also taking with him all the spiritually valuable portions of the Old Dispensation.

It is true that there is ethnic intolerance all through Israel's history, and that at times this intolerance was a major tragedy—for example in the exclusion of the Samaritans from fellowship with the community of Jerusalem on its return from exile. There is ample evidence of this intolerance during the first century in Palestine where (apart from the Samaritan issue) it had some genuine justification in the pressure of the heathen world on Jewish life. But ethnic intolerance was never less important in Jewish history than in the milieu in which Paul lived and worked. There are more references to proselytism than to exclusiveness in what Greek and Roman literature have to say on Diaspora Jewry; and, as we can see from Acts, Christianity spread to Gentiles through the Gentiles attracted to the synagogues; almost every reference to Paul's synagogue preaching refers to the presence of Greeks as well as Jews among his audiences; and nowhere is it one of the charges his enemies make against him that he is violating the ethnic exclusiveness of Israel. In fact, in the Diaspora synagogue of this period the conception of the family of Israel was just beginning to pass from a purely ethnic to a religious interpretation of the significance of Israel as the recipient of the divine promises and the bearer of a divine mission. In this milieu the universalism of Paul's message would not in itself compel him to break with Judaism or the Jewish community, however much it demanded new developments within the community to which the way was already open. If the majority of the members were not prepared for them, it was not because they could not accept fellowship with men born Gentiles, but because they did not agree with Paul that Jesus was the Messiah.

As in the previous chapter was the case with regard to Jesus of Nazareth, so in this it is, therefore, reasonable to say that in concentrating attention on the controversial aspects of Paul's relations with Judaism we are dealing with the fringes and not the heart of his message. The great space which controversies about the Law occupy in his letters might cause us to think otherwise, did we not reflect on the dangers as well as the advantages of knowing a man from his letters. They give a unique insight into his character, mind and temperament, but they do not necessarily reflect the general balance of his teaching, unless they are deliberately written for such a purpose, and even then they are likely to lack the careful choice of words and arguments one would demand in a theological treatise. In the case of Paul we have two groups of letters. Some were written during his missionary journeys (to the Thessalonians, the Galatians, the Romans and the Corinthians), and their authenticity has rarely been questioned. The only exceptions are parts of his letters to the Thessalonians, which have no particular importance for our purpose, since the arguments about the Law occur mainly in Galatians, Romans and Corinthians. A second group dates from the time of his imprisonment in Rome (to the Ephesians, Colossians and

Philippians and the personal letter to Philemon), and the authenticity of these has been doubted by many scholars, both because of differences in style and temper and because they reflect a more developed theology.

In spite of all the arguments which have been produced against these later letters, I confess myself still a believer in their authenticity. Partly, I do not believe that any work of creative genius would pass the tests evolved by a good deal of modern scholarship; and we have to accept that books which have survived the passage of time as have the works of the Bible are works of creative genius. No man could produce a book with the freshness of the Gospel of Mark, the history of the activities of the Apostles, or the letters of Paul by the curious combination of pedantry, distortion, copying and faking which some Biblical commentators seem to think the method by which great literature is created; and did any man produce a work by such methods these same commentators would be the first to discover that it was a patent and artificial forgery. Partly, as a historian, I am aware of how rapidly and convincingly these schools of criticism succeed and contradict each other. But partly also I find it quite incredible that there existed a contemporary of Paul, whose identity is absolutely unknown to us, who was capable of producing letters of such depth and beauty that he must be reckoned an even greater spiritual genius than the Apostle himself.

The arguments about the Law are mainly to be found in the group Galatians–Romans–Corinthians, and this group contains the one letter which comes nearest to being a general treatise, the letter to the Romans, the only Pauline letter written to a church with which Paul had not hitherto been in personal contact. The others primarily deal with particular matters which had arisen, and were uppermost in the Apostle's mind, at the time of writing. In the second group there are chance references to the Law, consistent with the attitude in the earlier letters, but they occupy a much smaller place. The most important letter is that to the Ephesians, which deals with the heart of Paul's message—

the life of the Christian "in Christ" and the meaning of those two words.

The impression which we get from these two groups of letters is confirmed by the speeches in the last chapters of Acts. There has been a shift of emphasis in the Apostle's mind, which would not prevent his accusers from launching their charge, but left the Apostle less interested in dealing with it. And if there be passages in the later letters reflecting the earlier controversies, so also in the earlier there is the same devotion to Christ to be found as in the later. And it is here that the real Paul is manifest, in the outpourings of adoration and devotion, of love and wonder, at the feet of Christ to be found in Ephesians, and not in the laboured argumentation of the earlier and longer letter to the Romans. The Paul of the trial speeches was concerned that men should know how he had found Christ, not what were his views upon the Law, even though the latter had been the reason for his first arrest.

So far as the person and office of Christ as Messiah are concerned, there is no question but that Paul thought of His significance as universal without the slightest distinction of Jew and Gentile. All equally had need of the two sides of His divine work. This dual pattern is made up, on the one side, of the risen Christ and, on the other, of the suffering and redeeming Christ. In both patterns there is a basic element which is Jewish, together with additions which are original to Paul, and may have their basis in the Hellenistic world in which Paul was born and worked. There were in his day many different and conflicting ideas among Jewish sects as to who the Messiah should be, and as to what should be his function. Paul's doctrine of the risen Christ as a pre-existent divine Being was familiar to some of the apocalyptists; and the relation of this risen Christ to His worshippers was developed by Paul (along the lines of the Midrashic and Alexandrian conception of the Adam Kadmon, the second or heavenly Adam) into the idea, familiar from many passages in his letters, of the Christ who is head of His body the Church, of which all Christians are the limbs.[41] Those

Jews who were disposed to accept Paul's identification of the Messiah with Jesus of Nazareth would not find it wholly strange for Paul to speak of Him in such terms.

More difficult to the Jewish mind were some of the ideas Paul drew from the historical fact of the Crucifixion. That the Messiah should be a priest was to be found in certain apocalyptic writings:[42] that He should be Himself the priestly sacrifice has its origin in the fifty-third chapter of Isaiah; but, so far as our evidence goes, a suffering Messiah only reappears in Jewish thought at a post-Pauline date. It is therefore more likely to have been influenced by Christian thought than to be the origin of such ideas among Christians.[43] On the other hand, such ideas lay very near to Paul's hands in the mystery religions, and in the conception of a dying and rising redeemer which originated in the "death" of Nature in the winter and its "resurrection" in the spring. Paul uses the word "Lord" to speak of Christ in the way in which these religions spoke of their redeemer, and the word has no natural origin in Jewish thought. But if there be some possibility, or even probability, that Paul took his *language* and even his *conception* from the mystery religions, the content which he gave to the idea was a product of his own Judeo-Christian background. The conception of "salvation" through the suffering of a redeemer god was one which is familiar in the later Roman Empire, and may indeed owe more to Christianity than the reverse; but the *longing for salvation* certainly existed in Paul's day and expressed itself in ideas which the Apostle could use, and which had the advantage of familiarity to his Gentile hearers. It was a world which, in the words of Vergil, "stretched out its hands in longing for the other shore."[44] On the formal side, Paul taught that men were by their nature alienated from God through sin, and needed a change of status, which they were themselves unable to achieve, before they could become acceptable to God. This change of status they obtained by an inner change in heart which resulted in faith in Christ. This was the "salvation," "justification" or "redemption" of which he spoke. Salvation was accompanied by the "imputation" of righteousness in return for faith. In the mystery religions this was the final goal. In Paul it is the first step. It is followed by union with the risen Christ in one body of which Christ is the Head, and in the living of a righteous life.

Some of the complications of Paul's attitude to the Law arise from the fact that the Law, i.e. Judaism, never set out to provide "justification" or "salvation" in the Pauline sense; but, on the other hand, it created a community within which was set forth the way of life in which men should live when justified. So Paul attacks it when it appears to be put forward as an alternative to salvation and denies that it can produce that result; while at the same time he admits it as holy, right and divine for men who, being justified, are then in a position to carry it out; and all his practical teaching is based upon it.

It was not with Jews that the question of the true basis of justification first became a practical issue. It arose within the Christian communities founded by Paul on his first missionary journey, communities which contained strong Gentile elements. Certain people, referred to as the "Judaisers" in Paul's letters, maintained that in order to be justified in the Pauline sense, these Gentiles must accept circumcision. They thus substituted a ritual initiation for the change of heart which Paul demanded. Since such an initiation was precisely what the mystery religions also required, this demand of the Judaisers would create in the minds of the Gentile members of the Church the belief that their religion was identical in character with other mystery religions, and offered spiritual and moral benefits in return for a purely ceremonial action. Paul was therefore dealing with a very real danger in combating the Judaisers, and he was doing it in a way which carried the official support of the Judeo-Christian Church. What was involved in this possible identification of Christianity with a mystery religion can best be seen from what happened at Corinth as a result of a mission in what we should call the "slums" of that cosmopolitan city. After a quarrel with the

Jews,[45] Paul spent eighteen months preaching among the Gentiles, and many were converted.[46] He then departed to Ephesus, where he was horrified to receive messengers from Corinth reporting that there was an appalling situation among his converts.[47]. Not only were they divided into bitterly partisan groups about the nature of the salvation which they had received,[48] but they considered that, being "saved," they were entitled to flout all moral and ethical commandments.[49] Paul's reply contained a thoroughly Jewish insistence on "works" and righteous living[50] as the way of life of those who had been redeemed in Christ.

Among the Jewish element of his hearers and followers the issue could not have arisen in this form. No Jew would have imagined that circumcision entitled him to lead a loose and immoral life. But Paul must have encountered the view among Jewish formalists that the mere fact of being a son of Abraham, and received into the Covenant by circumcision, was itself a guarantee that a Jew would have his share of the world to come. Such a belief was not sanctioned by true Judaism, but it enjoyed a popular existence in later times, and may well have been found in Diaspora synagogues. The Matthean version of the message of John the Baptist, "think not to say within yourselves, We have Abraham to our father: for I say unto you, that God is able of these stones to raise up children unto Abraham,"[51] shows that it was current in the first century.

In any case, Paul would certainly have met many Jews who, while not taking any such mechanical view of their privileges, saw no need for, and felt no particular interest in, a Messiah of Paul's variety. It is unfortunate that we have very little information as to the form of Paul's preaching to, and discussion with, Jews. For, whereas with Gentiles he had to persuade those who enjoyed being saved that they must also accept the harder task of living moral lives, with Jews his argument would have had to follow the opposite tack. They accepted the need to lead moral lives and Paul's task was to convince them they could not do this without the "grace" which came from acceptance of the Messiah. Through Him, "all that believe are justified from all things from which ye could not be justified by the Law of Moses."[52] For this had been Paul's own Jewish experience.

Normal Jewish experience would suggest that the equivalent of "justification before God" was the *consequence* of a life lived according to the Law, not the *initiation* into such a life; whereas much of Paul's language would certainly suggest the opposite; and certain Christian schools of thought of a predestinarian kind have built their whole doctrine of salvation on a mechanical interpretation of this idea. If it is really Paul's doctrine that justification by faith replaces the need to seek to lead a life obedient to the Law of God, then indeed the break with Judaism was complete; and Paul had no moral right to follow the line he adopted in his defences. But there is no suggestion of any such idea in Paul's teaching; and if his argument to Jews was that they needed grace from the Messiah to live the life their Judaism called them to live, then that might be a matter for controversy, made more difficult by the expressions Paul had introduced from his Gentile environment, but it is no evidence of a break with Judaism. It is still a *Jewish* Messiah he was presenting to them. Moreover, though Paul did not believe that circumcision could bring justification, he certainly considered it essential as the entry into the Covenant relationship between God and the Jewish people; and he held that Jewish Christians should continue to observe the whole Law, except in so far as it involved separation in religion from Gentile Christians.

In the strong opposition which Paul expresses between the ideas of "justification by faith" and "justification by works" both Christian and Jewish scholars have seen an intentional opposition between Christianity and Judaism. The former have used his words as a justification for the complete abandonment or even condemnation of the religion of Sinai; and the latter have been shocked by the injustice and even apparent ignorance of the nature of Torah shown in his attack. Both have ignored the setting

in which Paul's words were written—that they arose out
of a practical issue concerning Gentile converts, and not
out of a general consideration of Judaism as practised by
Jews, even though, as we shall see later, there are portions
of the argument dealing with this subject.

The opposition "faith" *versus* "works" is not one which
would naturally spring to the mind of any Jewish teacher
addressing any Jewish audience. There is no evidence that
such issues as atheism and agnosticism troubled the Jewish
mind at that time. The Jews were conditioned to accept
without question the doctrine that God exists and that He
cares for Israel. The Jewish teacher could assume faith
in God as a genuine conviction of his audience. His teaching
dealt with men's response to this belief. Consequently,
when he was concerned to correct interest in externals
or undue emphasis on the merit accorded to works, he did
it by stressing joy, trust and love as the motives for fulfilling
the will of God revealed in the Commandments. Paul
was dealing with a different situation in addressing audiences
containing Gentiles to whom the idea of faith in a God who
sought personal relations with His creatures was new and
strange. He had first to teach a new conception of God,
then teach faith in Him as a basis of personal relations
between God and men, and he had continually to stress the
importance of this teaching. He had also to prevent a
subsequent escape by his converts into a formal acquiescence
or a ceremonial response. Both dangers were very real;
for we must remember that Paul's converts would become
members of what was still a Jewish sect. They would meet,
many for the first time, with all the external practices of
Judaism, clean and unclean meats, Sabbath observances,
and so on, and would easily be fascinated into thinking
that these were the central aspects of "the Law," and strict
observance of them the main task of a Christian—just as
strict observance of its ritual was the main task of the
adherent of the mystery religions.

Though it is not directly relevant to Paul's intentions,
it is pertinent to add that if we change the opposites from

'faith" and "works" as bases of salvation to "faith" and "joy, trust and love" as motives for the service of God, we do then reach a real distinction between Judaism and Christianity, as they have historically developed. If we consider God and humanity as the two poles between which creation grows, the Christian emphasis on man's faith has constantly directed the Christian gaze at the divine pole. The Christian is constantly urged to concern himself with the nature and attributes of God Himself; and the result has been the strong theological emphasis running through Christian history—its innumerable theological controversies, its heresies and schisms, its stress on orthodoxy in belief. The Jewish gaze has been fixed on spiritual motives, but as they affect the human pole. For joy, trust and love are human responses to an accepted and unquestioned conception of and belief in the Divine.

It is, of course, true that this generalisation of the two religions does not cover the whole of the facts. There is theology in Judaism; and there is concern with the human response in Christianity. But it at least covers so much of the facts that there has been a *tendency* in each religion to think that the side which it emphasises is the only one. That in Paul's own lifetime there were Christians who thought that faith alone mattered we can see from the letter of James, passages of which definitely take up actual arguments used by Paul: [53]

"What doth it profit, my brethren, though a man say he hath faith, and have not works? can faith save him? If a brother or sister be naked, and destitute of daily food, and one of you say unto them, Depart in peace, be ye warmed and filled; notwithstanding ye give them not those things which are needful to the body; what doth it profit? Even so faith, if it hath not works, is dead, being alone. But wilt thou know, O vain man, that faith without works is dead? Was not Abraham our father justified by works, when he had offered Isaac his son upon the altar? [54] Seest thou how faith wrought with his works, and by works was faith made perfect? And the scripture was fulfilled which saith, Abraham believed God, and it was imputed unto him for righteousness: and he was called the Friend of God. Ye see then how that by works a man is justified, and not by faith only. Likewise also was not Rahab the harlot justified by works, when she had received the messengers, and had sent them out another way? For as the body without the spirit is dead, so faith without works is dead also."

And the same false emphasis as James here attacks recurs in the famous Paulinists of Christian history from Augustine through Luther to Karl Barth. So strong has been the Christian tradition on this subject that in the Thirty-nine Articles of Religion of the Anglican Church, which are a product of the religious controversies of the sixteenth century, the third of the four articles dealing with "works" says of good works done before justification (by faith): [55]

"Works done before the grace of Christ, and the Inspiration of His Spirit, are not pleasant to God, forasmuch as they spring not of faith in Jesus Christ, neither do they make men meet to receive grace . . . yea rather, for that they are not done as God has willed and commanded them to be done, we doubt not that they have the nature of sin."

While the historical origin of the argument lay in the issue raised by the Judaisers, it would be wrong to say that the whole matter ended here, and that Paul made no demands upon his Jewish hearers except to add belief in Jesus as Messiah to their existing Judaism. Paul's attitude towards Jews starts from the same point as that of Jesus expressed in the controversies with the Pharisees. But it was sharpened by his own experience as a Jew. Jesus reproached Pharisaism with the danger that their insistence on externals would be taken by their hearers as offering a substitute for obedience to God; Paul, as one whom William James calls a "twice-born," had found himself psychologically unable to live according to the Law just because of its emphasis on laws. It is important to remember that this is an exposure of a weakness in institutional Jewish developments more than an attack on the contents of Judaism itself. The Torah is "holy and the commandment holy and just and good."[56] But Paul had not only found himself unable to obey it, but, instead, doing things he hated. What Paul has to say is as applicable to the regulations in Paul's own Christianity as to anything in Judaism; and the problem of how such men find an inspiration leading to moral action is basically psychological and not religious. Any worthy object which acts as an internal inspiration instead of an external goad might supply the necessary incentive. For Paul the change had been effected by his discovery of Christ; and he was convinced that the same was true for all Jews. Faith in Christ would secure the inner feeling of "justification" which the works of the Law could not secure. But faith in Christ meant acceptance of the victory which had been won by Christ over the sin which prevented them from obeying the Law, and also the recognition that "in Christ" man became a "new creature" with new possibilities. Jew and Gentile were thus on the same footing; and, from an ideal standpoint, Paul could say that for the Christian Jew the laws of Judaism were no longer necessary. Faith and the love that went with it would produce spontaneously lives such as the Law sought vainly to produce.

It is in following out this argument that Paul's letters contain statements which would justify the charge of the Jerusalem rioters. For here he is dealing, not with the method of initiation into the Christian life, but with the whole manner of living; and there are remarks, especially in Romans and Galatians, which still rightly give offence to the Jewish reader, and would have given similar offence to his Jewish hearers. For they undoubtedly appear to deal with the whole of Judaism in a manner a Jew cannot accept as just or historically true. There are three passages in particular of this kind, and the interesting point about

Djc

them is that they are mutually inconsistent. There is no such inconsistency in Paul's doctrine of the Messiah, or in his conviction that no ceremonial act could take the place of faith in Christ; so that we are justified in assuming that they are of lesser importance in his eyes. They had not been so carefully and deeply thought out, and this could only mean that they were not in his mind the basis on which he took so definite a step as that supposed by his accusers and so many of his Jewish and Christian interpreters, and abandoned Judaism for Christianity.

The transition is provided by a passage in Galatians in which Paul speaks of the Law as a schoolmaster to bring us to Christ.[57] Once we have been received by Christ we no longer need it, because we already know its precepts and follow them out of love, needing no external pressure. This can be considered an entirely Jewish interpretation of the times of the Messiah. It is a repetition of Jeremiah's belief in a time when the Law would be "put in the inward parts and written in the heart."[58] There is nothing in it to give offence, though it would naturally not be accepted by Jews who did not regard Christ as Messiah. But this would not be true of the elaborate and involved argument in Romans in which both Jew and Gentile are put on the same footing, awaiting the revelation of the goodness of God in Christ, the Gentile without law, the Jew under a law he could not obey, so that both Jew and Gentile should feel the need for Christ. That the Law was given solely in order that man might know himself a sinner through his inability to keep it is an interpretation which no Jew could accept; and it is even more strongly put in a passage in Galatians where Paul says:[59] "for as many as are of the works of the law are under the curse: for it is written, Cursed is every one that continueth not in all things which are written in the book of the law to do them"; and repeats it later[60] by insisting that to accept any of the law is to accept the whole, and, since man cannot possibly fulfil the whole law perfectly, its acceptance damns him more irretrievably than if he had never known it, unless he accepts Christ "who has become a curse for him." The argument conforms to no known Jewish interpretation of Torah, but, what is more important, it involves a totally inacceptable picture of God turning the creation into a self-centred melodrama which mocks the reality of the human tragedy it involves. But that the idea lingered in the mind of the Apostle for, at any rate, some part of his ministry is shown by the fact that he repeats it in the second letter to the Corinthians, where he speaks of the Law as "the ministration of death, written and engraven in stones,"[61] and now abolished. If Paul said similar things in his sermons and verbal controversies, and said them frequently, then it is not surprising that the Jews of Asia spoke of him as one who taught them to "forsake Moses." But did they in fact form an essential and permanent part of Paul's teaching? Is it possible to assume that, even though the Jews of Asia had remembered them, Paul himself had forgotten them? So long as we are not obliged to assume that the Apostle lacked all human weaknesses, or that every saying of his was carefully weighed and fully integrated into a consistent whole, nothing is more reasonable to assume than that he had in fact forgotten secondary portions of a past controversy. The relation of the ceremonial Law to Salvation remained of permanent importance with him. Salvation could only come by faith in Christ. But what other arguments he had developed as support of this thesis he may well have forgotten.

There is one other matter which needs treatment. In Rom. ix–xi, Paul deals not with the religious so much as with the national issue, not with a possible antithesis between "Christianity" and "Judaism," but with a real antithesis between Jews and Gentiles. To understand this we need to consider the situation of the first Jewish-Christian communities. Among the many different views which were then held as to the nature of the expected Messiah, it is extremely doubtful if any Jews thought it possible that when the Messiah came he would not be instantly recognised, but would have to win the acceptance of men one by one. The idea of a secret Messiah is a later one in Judaism.

Yet this is what the believers saw happening around them and it left them bewildered. We can see, looking back, that the claims made by Jesus of Nazareth were such that it would be only by individual action that men would accept or reject Him; but to them it was difficult to understand. They could not have held the view subsequently universally held by the Christian Church that "the Jews" had rejected Him, for most of them were themselves Jews, and other Jews were daily coming into the fold. But there was no question but that the Jewish leaders and the bulk of the Jewish people were hostile or indifferent; and, on the other hand, it was evident in experience that many Gentiles were accepting Him. That this latter was not wholly unexpected has already been shown, though even here men may not have expected that Gentiles would come to accept the Jewish Messiah, not by a national act, but one by one. This is the situation which Paul seeks to explain in these chapters. The argument is complicated, as are all arguments which try to combine predestinarianism with men's free will; and Paul had inherited from his Pharisaic background a strongly predestinarian view of the relation of God with His creation. Over the various arguments to prove that there is no inconsistency in the divine promises made to Abraham, and that God can do as He will, we need not linger; they deal with the kind of problem any predestinarian has to deal with, in the way any predestinarian deals with them; and they are as unconvincing as any similar presentation to one who is not a predestinarian. Of more interest is his explanation of why the bulk of Israel had not accepted his Messiah.

First of all he deals with the question historically. He quotes the prophets to show that it was never expected that more than a remnant of Israel would prove to be faithful; and here he denies categorically the commonly held Jewish belief that the mere fact of physical descent from Abraham was enough to make a Jew superior to Gentiles and an automatic heir to the promises made to Abraham. Paul insists on the equality of Jew and Gentile before God. But while this disposes of "bad Jews," he still has to explain why "good Jews" do not already possess all the necessary qualifications for inheritance. It is here that there is the clearest opposition in Paul's words between "faith" and "works" where "works" must primarily cover the practice of Judaism by Jews, and is in no way concerned with the terms of admission of Gentiles to the Christian community. If it were not for Acts and the many passages where "works" are condemned in connection with his Gentile converts, to whom he was constantly urging the practice of works in the sense of morality and righteous living (so that works must mean ceremonial as an alternative to faith), the traditional view that Paul had wholly abandoned Judaism could be held to be established by such a passage as "being ignorant of God's righteousness, and seeking to establish their own, they did not subject themselves to the righteousness of God. For Christ is the end of the law unto righteousness to every one that believeth."[62] It links on to the condemnations of the Law which have been quoted from Galatians; but it is also linked to the condemnation of laws—with a small "l"—in the preceding chapter (Chapter vii), and to Paul's preoccupation with status before God. There is nothing anywhere in his letters or in Acts to suggest that Paul ever considered that physical descent could establish such a status; there is nothing to suggest that there were any limits to the universality of his claim that status depended on faith in Christ. It was as valid for Jews as for Gentiles. But this still leaves open the issue as to how a man was to live once the question of his status was regulated by faith in Christ, and there, against the few passages in which he appears to condemn Judaism as the basis of living, is the much greater evidence that he considered the way of life of Judaism to be the basis even for his Gentile converts and the whole Law the basis for himself and Jewish Christians.

The chapters end with the famous analogy of the grafted olive, in which Paul tries to meet the puzzlement of the Christian community as to why the Messiah had not been recognised. Abandoning elaborate argument and giving

full rein to his love for his people, both Jew and Gentile,
he suggests that in the divine purpose "a hardening in part
hath befallen Israel"[63] in order to give time to the Gentiles
to come into the Messianic community as full and equal
partners. Then, when "the fulness of the Gentiles be come
in . . ." all Israel shall be saved. It is on this note of hope
that the section ends. The subsequent history of this belief
of Paul has considerable importance; it was used by the
medieval papacy to protect the Jews from forcible baptism
or complete extermination at the hands of Christians;
for, it was argued, the divine plan required that some Jews
survive as Jews to usher in the return of the Messiah.

To form the whole picture, we need to set the actual
words and arguments of Paul against the background of the
life of his little communities within the framework of
Diaspora Judaism. Accustomed as we are to the completely
separate existence of Church and Synagogue, it is difficult to
realise how completely Jewish was the environment of these
earliest Christian communities. Officially, it was their in-
corporation into the privileges accorded by the Romans to
the Jewish people that permitted them to avoid any participation in the official paganism around them. It was not
until after the separation that the Christians were liable to
persecution as an unincorporated and unlicensed religious
brotherhood which refused to share in the official worship of
the State. But their participation in Jewish life went far
beyond this official link, which would usually have been
relatively unimportant, so long as few men of wealth or
members of the army were to be found in the Christian
community. Though their relations were doubtless often
marked by controversies and even at times by official action
against them on the part of the synagogue authorities (particularly a generation or two later), they existed as one of the
many groups of which a Jewish community was composed.
They had their own elders, their own special meetings for
worship and fellowship, but they also shared in the worship
and fellowship of the synagogue, where their Gentile members would doubtless have been considered on the same

footing as the other Gentiles who were partially or wholly identified with its life. Paul himself was living a thoroughly Jewish life, hurrying from his missionary work to take part in the feasts at Jerusalem, observing the ceremonial law, and earning his living by a trade in accordance with Jewish custom. The teaching he was giving them as to their way of life was identical with much of what they would have learnt in the readings and sermons of the synagogue. His method of argument identified him with other rabbinic teachers. He could refer easily and casually to the patriarchs and great figures of Jewish history because they would have been already made familiar with them in synagogue worship. Such an identification meant far more than familiarity with a certain set of laws and regulations; it meant intimate participation in a whole way of life, totally different from anything they would have known in the pagan world around them. If they felt separated from other members of the synagogue, Greek or Jewish, on the tremendously important issue of their Messianic faith, yet they were still closer to them than to any other group. In such circumstances, had Paul really wished to separate his flock from Jewry, and make a complete religious break, he would have had to make his meaning very much clearer than anything which is contained in his letters. And it is probably true to add that in any case many of his converts may have understood little of the more complicated arguments which he used. Paul himself says of his churches that they contained "not many wise, not many mighty, not many noble," so that it is not surprising if aspects of his teaching either provided a fruitful source of misunderstanding or passed entirely over their heads. There is one verse of Galatians to which theologians (so I was told by my professor when I was a student) have given 430 separate explanations: "now a mediator is not a mediator of one, but God is one."[64] What could the unfortunate Galatians have made of it?

Paul's permanent contribution to the spiritual pilgrimage of humanity is his Christocentric mysticism. As surely as Isaiah is the product of the continuing activity of Sinai, so is

Paul that of the continuing activity of Calvary. He is the
"new creature" made possible by the dynamic power of
divine action taking place once again in the space and time
of history. Doubtless his sense of the nearness of the End and
the powerlessness of man by himself lent urgency to his
sense of human need; they can explain why he would like to
lose himself in the divine; they cannot explain what happened when he did. His sense of union with Christ in a new
outpouring of power pervades and illumines all he writes,
even when as formal theology it is most obscure or untenable. And this sense of union goes far beyond an individual
benefit. He sees the whole Church in Christ who is its Head,
united in an intimacy of personal relationship between
Creator and creature which goes beyond Hillel's great
declaration that the whole of the Law is comprised in love
of God and love of neighbour. That declaration still leaves
God, man and neighbour as three separate entities in themselves. In Paul they become one—God and man, man and
his neighbour—in the Christ in whom "dwelleth all the fulness
of the Godhead bodily."[65] All humanity is inevitably included in that centre in which are neither bond nor free,
neither Jew nor Greek, but all are one in Christ.[66] Through
the action of God Himself, the whole creation is reconciled
and restored to its original perfection, not negatively, as in
some Eastern mystics, but positively in the outpouring of
divine love, filling the innermost recesses of the human
personality, and flowing back to God, and outwards into
creative life through the complete surrender of the human
soul itself to this divine filling.

This mystical exaltation of Paul's led him not to retire
from the world in order to contemplate the Godhead, but to
lead a life of continuous activity, of utter indifference to
sickness, exhaustion and danger, in passionate longing to
bring to others something of the joy and peace that over-
flowed in his own soul.

Paul's historical contribution to the growth of the Christian
Church has been different, and its value more debatable.
On the fundamental issue of faith as opposed to works or

ritual as the basis of entry into the Christian life he failed completely. By infant baptism the Church restored just what he sought to destroy. A ritual act, by being called sacramental, does not necessarily become an act of faith—particularly in the case of a new-born infant; and baptism was supposed to do exactly what "faith in Christ" was believed to do by Paul. It changed the child's status and made it "a child of God, a member of Christ, and an inheritor of the Kingdom of Heaven," instead of "a child of sin." [67] Likewise the Church, as it developed its organisation, evolved new laws of conduct precisely of the kind which Paul had found incapable of securing right living; and when it gained political power in the fourth century A.D., it extended the rôle of compulsion from matters of conduct even to matters of faith; and Christian Emperors, egged on by the ecclesiastical hierarchy, imperially forbad heresy to exist, and killed and persecuted those who did not comply. It needed a barbarian king, Theodoric the Goth, to make the wise pronouncement, when asked to legislate against Judaism, that he could not command belief in men's hearts. [68]

For these two failures it would be unjust to blame Paul. But what is one to say of the effects of his teaching about Judaism on the subsequent history of the Jewish people? The bare fact is that nearly two thousand years of Jewish history owe their sufferings more to the writings of Paul than to any other individual outside the evangelists. In both cases it was not the effect which the author intended. Paul certainly would have been horrified to hear the pitiful travesty of Judaism which Christian teachers, having no contact with it themselves, taught and still teach on the basis of what they have understood him to say. The Jewish background of which he was so proud is quoted as evidence that he knew fully of what he was writing; and, so long as the Scriptures were held to be free from human error, so long it was not possible to argue that here he was carried away by his zeal, here he said more than he meant, here heaven alone knew what it was he was trying to say. It is the Paulinists rather than Paul himself who bear the direct responsibility; and at

least one can say of Paul that he was not responsible for the
doctrine of Scriptural authority which elevated letters,
written sometimes in haste and based on local conditions, to
so intolerable an inerrancy. At least Paul does not charge the
Jews with responsibility for the Crucifixion. As that charge
moves into the centre of the picture, the blame shifts to the
interpreters of the evangelists. But in so far as the Church
has wholly misunderstood Judaism, we must remember that
the letters of Paul were written before the Gospels. The
standard was already set when the latter were written. One
can only say that, like Paul, they did not realise that they
were writing what later ages would consider verbally in-
spired Scriptures, containing nothing but truth and nothing
less than the whole of truth.

Paul's failure to produce a permanent Judeo-Christian
Church was due, however, primarily to his mystical absorption in his Messiah. The Judaism which he personally, in
his life, combined with this absorption, was never consistently and fully worked out in his writings, and the unity
of the Gentile and the Jew in Christ was never integrated
into a philosophy of the meaning and application of Torah
in the Gentile world. The compromise which he found satis-
factory in his own experience could have lasted only through
a transitional period such as that in which he lived. As the
Church settled down, the system of a different scheme of life
for Jewish and Gentile Christians, which yet implied no in-
equality of status, must have given way to some agreed
foundation for all, and the result would have been that
shifting of emphasis in the interpretation of Torah which is
implied in the teaching of Jesus. The theory that there is a
fundamental opposition between His teaching and that of
Paul will not bear critical examination. On one side it
relies too much on a watering down of the conflict between
Jesus and the Pharisees. On the other, it implies that Paul
intended deliberately to create the situation which led to the
rupture between the two religions, by creating a theological
and ecclesiastical system which Judaism would not, and
could not, tolerate. It is true that Paul was in fact the prime

author of the doctrines which made a separation inevitable. But that is a very different matter from stating that such was his purpose.

Both Jesus and Paul lived within the Jewish way of life; both rejected the place which the ceremonial law and the interpretations of the Pharisees were coming to occupy in Judaism. The differences between them are explicable by the differences in their situation. Paul was living primarily in the Hellenistic world; Jesus in the Judaic. A large section of Paul's teaching was inevitably concerned with the Person of Jesus, whereas this occupies a very small place in the synoptic, or public, teaching of Jesus. Paul was concerned with the effect of ceremonial on his Gentile converts: Jesus was concerned with the danger of stressing externals to ordinary Jews.

We find Jesus saying "there is nothing from without a man that entering into him can defile him; but the things which come out of him those are they that defile the man,"[69] and some texts of Mark add the Pauline comment: "this he said making all meats clean."[70] Jesus condemns those that[71] "tithe mint and anise and cummin, and have left undone the weightier matters of the law, judgment, and mercy and faith." But he adds: "These ought ye to have done, and not to leave the other undone." And at the same time we find Jesus quoting the Law and the prophets as freely as Paul in his ethical and moral teaching. He quotes the two great commandments as the gateway to the Kingdom of Heaven, and He says of the Law that[72] "till heaven and earth pass, one jot or one tittle shall in no wise pass from the law, till all be fulfilled."

It is wrong therefore to say that there is a fundamental contradiction between Jesus and Paul. But Paul himself must be held primarily responsible for the fact that instead of a gradual and peaceful development, without schism, a violent break between the two faiths took place. Out of the mass of his teaching on the subject, the simple Gentile Christians of his day retained only two ideas about Judaism, both of which rested on the belief that there was nothing in

it apart from a set of ceremonial and ethical laws for individual conduct. Sometimes one, sometimes the other, is
uppermost in the succeeding centuries. On the one hand is
the idea that the whole Torah was "a schoolmaster to bring
us to Christ" and that its further functioning is now super-
fluous. This view finds endorsement in the Epistle to the
Hebrews. But the other idea is that Torah is no more than a
set of external rules, which never produced a spiritual result;
and this idea played an even larger rôle in the critical years
of controversy which preceded the separation of the two
religions, and dominated the aggressive attitude of Gentile
Christians to their fellow Christians of the Judean Church.
It is based on a confusion between Paul's condemnation of
external ritual as a source of "justification" before God, and
his proclamation of the failure of rules of conduct to secure a
change of heart. From such passages the Gentile Christians
decided that any conformity with the Law was sin, and
excluded Judeo-Christians from the fellowship of the
Church. This situation is revealed in a passage of Justin's
Dialogue with Trypho, written about a hundred years later:[73]

"And Trypho again inquired, 'But if someone, knowing
that this is so, after he recognises that this man is Christ,
and has believed in and obeys him, wishes however to
observe these (institutions), will he be saved?'

"I said, 'In my opinion, Trypho, such an one will be
saved, if he does not strive in every way to persuade other
men—I mean those Gentiles who have been circumcised
from error by Christ, to observe the same things as himself, telling them that they will not be saved unless they
do so. This you did yourself at the commencement of the
discourse, when you declared that I would not be saved
unless I observe these institutions.'

"Then he replied, 'Why then have you said, "In my
opinion, such an one will be saved", unless there are some
who affirm that such will not be saved?'

"There are such people, I answered; and these do not
venture to have any intercourse with or to extend hospi-
tality to such persons; but I do not agree with them."

It is normal in the story of a schism from an existing faith to find that the first moves—whether intentionally or not—are taken by the innovators. Until some action or pronouncement compels them to take action the leaders of the older faith are not likely to take to strong measures. So it was in the schism between Christianity and Judaism. The difficulties came from the leaders of the new group. It is not difficult to understand why Paul roused antagonism as well as enthusiasm in the synagogues of the Diaspora. He was a man towards whom it would be difficult to be neutral. Once one accepted his identification of the Messiah with Jesus of Nazareth, the rest of his views could be understood, though there were some even then who challenged them. But, once acceptance of Jesus of Nazareth came to involve also acceptance of what ordinary men could understand of Paul's attitude to Torah, then the opposition was bound to become violent; and all the evidence is that in the next generation the Gentile Christians aggressively proclaimed their understanding and misunderstanding of Paul's complicated attitude to the Law. Such a situation explains the confused but persistent presence in the traditions of the later Church of a violent persecution at the hands of the Jews. As I have shown in *The Conflict of Church and Synagogue*, nearly all the stories can be traced to memories of the period before Bar Cochba, and they contain nothing inherently improbable.[74] The synagogue of the Diaspora possessed certain powers in dealing with religious offences, and there is every probability that they were used against adherents of the new heresy.

Meanwhile, the Judeo-Christians, where they formed separate Churches of their own, as in Palestine, lived a more or less peaceful life. It cannot be said that they were looked upon with favour, but they were rarely disturbed. Apart from the murder—or execution—of James in 62[75] no judicial action is known to have been taken against them, until their fellowship with the nascent churches of the Diaspora brought the whole matter within the scope of Jochanan ben Zakkai and the Jabne group's policy towards all dissidents. This was in the last decades of the first century, and until then it seems that they continued to share in common worship in the synagogue with other Jews. In any case the first step towards their exclusion from this fellowship was the inclusion in synagogue worship of a new Benediction, or rather Malediction, on the "Nazarenes." As we know that the author of this Malediction was Samuel the Small, a contemporary of Gamaliel II, we can date it to the period between 80 and 100. At about the same time, or a little later, a formal condemnation of the Nazarenes was drawn up by the Sanhedrin, and circulated officially to the synagogues of the Diaspora.[76] We have many references to this document in Christian literature from the middle of the second century onwards, and its most likely date is some time before the revolt of Bar Cochba. We have not its text, but it denounced Jesus of Nazareth as a deceiver and excommunicated his followers from membership of the synagogues.

It is difficult to assess the political, as apart from the religious, effect of this denunciation. The security of the earliest Christian communities *vis-à-vis* the Roman authorities lay in their membership of the Synagogue, and their participation thereby in the privileges enjoyed by the Jews, particularly exemption from any act which would involve religious compromise—work on the Sabbath, worship of other gods, and so on. Christians would need these exemptions as much as Jews; and by the time of Pliny (Governor of Bithynia in A.D. 111) we find that they no longer possessed them.[77] But they were an obscure sect, and it is highly probable that they had been separately organised for several decades before the time of Pliny. They would have become one of the many unincorporated, but not "illegal," communities of the Empire, or possibly a community licensed for the burial rites of its members.

So long as the conflict was internal to the Synagogue the main subject of controversy was the Law. Once it became a conflict between separately organised Jews and Christians, the field shifted a good deal. The Promises in the Old Testament, and the interpretation of the many passages held to be Messianic forecasts, became more prominent. As a Jewish sect, Christians could share the Old Testament with other Jews; as a separate religion they came more and more to demand its exclusive ownership, and this at a time when the Jews had lost Temple and Holy City. The disastrous defeat of the revolt of Bar Cochba had reduced the Jews to a status as humble as that of the unlicensed Christian communities. In fact in some ways they were worse off, and if, fifty years before, Jews were in a position to denounce Christians, and sometimes did so, now the situation was reversed, and Christians could and did denounce Jews.

There is nothing for either religion to be proud of in the half-century or more during which their separation from each other was achieved. As a Christian, I am more concerned with confession of the most un-Christian conduct of my Christian predecessors, and, in the long run, it was the Christian behaviour which mattered. For their power to inflict harm on their Jewish opponents became far greater than any power of persecution possessed by the Jews. It is with that unhappy story, prolonged through nearly two thousand years of Christian history, that I shall be concerned in the following chapter.

Part Three

HISTORICAL DEVELOPMENTS

CHAPTER FOUR

THE TRADITIONAL ATTITUDE OF CHRISTIANITY TO JUDAISM

DURING THE FIRST CENTURY, many Jews entered the nascent Church, and the bulk of the leaders of the local churches were Jewish. But the situation changed rapidly as the first century drew to a close. As the Christian groups in the Diaspora came to outnumber in importance those in Palestine, so Gentile Christians came to be more prominent than Jewish. Under the influence of Paul's letters, and of the violent controversies they had engendered, the issue, for those Jews who for one reason or another were attracted to Christianity, came to be not merely, Do you accept Jesus as Messiah? but: Do you accept Jesus as Messiah in the sense that He has put an end to Torah as a way of life based on a permanent divine revelation? By the time of Justin Martyr (*c*. 150) the Church was in process of rejecting the Apostolic position of the earliest days, and was coming to consider the Judeo-Christians as heretics. And more and more the Jewish refusal to consider this condition, which prevented Jews from becoming Judeo-Christians, prevented them also from considering the basic question of the Messiahship of Jesus. The Gentile Christian would not, of course, have put this question explicitly as it is put above. He was convinced that the Church had understood and retained all that was essential in the Old Testament as a "schoolmaster to bring us to Christ," and that the Jewish interpretation of the Torah was utterly wrong. In fact, the Christian misunderstanding of the nature of the Old Testament was from the beginning, and still is, one of the main causes of Christian

misunderstanding of the nature of Judaism. An expansion
of the argument used by Paul in Galatians will show what
later ages could make of the material he provided. Agobard,
Archbishop of Lyons in the ninth century, thus describes
the curse which lies on those who observe the Law:[1]

"All who are under the Law are under a curse, and are
clothed with the curse as with a garment. It [the curse]
has entered, like water, inside them, and like oil into their
bones. They are, moreover, cursed in the city, and cursed
in the field; cursed in coming in, and cursed in going out;
cursed in the fruits of the womb, the land and the flock;
cursed are their cellars, their barns, their medicines, their
food, and the crumbs that drop from it, and none of them
can escape from this appalling, this ghastly, curse of the
Law, except by Him who was made a curse for us."

The controversy of the Church with the Jews about the
Old Testament has been expressed since the earliest days in
an immense mass of literature. It begins with the "testi-
monies to the Messiah" and continues under various titles,
such as *Altercatio cum Judaeo*, *Adversus Judaeos*, right into
modern times. This literature was only partially intended to
convert Jews to Christianity. To a very large extent it was
intended to guard the Christian flock against Jewish criticism or Jewish condemnation of the conventional Christian
interpretation of Old Testament passages. This is shown by
the care with which new converts, during their instruction
in the Christian faith, were warned against the rival views
which Jews might put forward.[2] The themes of this literature
were pre-ordained by the subject, and there is astonishingly
little variety in the greater part of it. Proofs from prophecy
that Jesus is the Messiah naturally occupy the central place.
The theme allowed of various developments. The prophecies
showed that it was pre-ordained that the Messiah should
suffer. One writer, Anastasius of Sinai (sixth century),
warned Jews that this would be true even if they were right
in believing that Jesus was not the Messiah, so that they
could only expect that should another come, they would

reject Him also.[3] Others developed the theme that prophecy could only be fulfilled once, so that there was no possibility that the expected Jewish Messiah could be anyone but Anti-Christ.[4] Some of the early renunciations imposed on Jews at baptism compelled the proselyte to renounce "the Antichrist whom all the Jews expect as Messiah."[5] Curiously enough this theme of Jewish expectation of a Messiah still to come was not often related to the Christian belief in the return of Jesus. The idea is faintly foreshadowed in Paul's letter to the Romans, but it does not reappear directly until the time of the Protestant millenarians in seventeenth-century England, who linked it to the return of the Jews to that country. Since prophecy said that the Messiah would gather the Jews from all lands, He could not come until they were scattered in all lands, and the English Government, by refusing them admission, was delaying His return.[6] The transition, however, is prepared in the intervening time by the compensation which Christians evolved for their lack of success in their efforts to convert Jews. The Scriptures said that they would not be converted until the Messiah came, at which time a remnant would be saved.

After the question of Jesus as Messiah came such subjects as the Doctrine of the Trinity, the rejection of the Jews and the election of the Church as the true Israel into its place. Later various matters of history and experience were added.

In view of the nature of this literature, it is not surprising to find that nearly all the material of Christian polemic before the Middle Ages shows very little knowledge of contemporary Jewish custom and belief. Its main sources were the denunciations of the prophets, and the exhortations and condemnations of the Law. The Jews were made to pay dearly for the unflattering honesty of their prophets and sages. Every weakness denounced, every failure exposed, every sin castigated, was seized on with relish by Christian preachers; while every word of praise or comfort was appropriated to its own history by the Christian Church. One of the most hideous examples of this is a series of sermons delivered by John Chrysostom (345–407) in the

Syrian Antioch in 387.[7] Chrysostom (the golden tongued) was the most famous orator of his day, as well as the most-read Bible commentator. His commentaries are still widely used in the Eastern Church. The sermons are an uninterrupted torrent of vituperation and abuse, of which the only basis appears to be the respect in which Jews were held in Antioch and the friendly relations which existed between them and the Christians. He finds nothing to attack in the ethical or social conduct of the Jews in question. All his abuse is based on the Bible. For example, on the basis of Ps. cvi, 35-7: "they were mingled among the heathen, and learned their works . . . and offered their sons and daughters to devils," he accused his Jewish contemporaries of this crime. Eusebius of Cæsarea (260–340), one of the most important Church historians of the fourth century, in two immense works, *Preparatio Evangelica* and *Demonstratio Evangelica*, based his whole treatment of the Jews on an artificial distinction between the words "Hebrew" and "Jew."[8] All the virtuous characters of the Old Testament, patriarchs, prophets and kings alike, he called Hebrews, and considered to be pre-incarnation Christians; all the evil characters he called Jews. Eusebius is important because he was one of the most influential figures at the time when the Church first acquired the power to reinforce her verbal denunciations by imperial legislation, of which there will be more to say later. Another writer of the fourth century who dealt extensively with Jewish matters was Epiphanius (*c.* 320–403), who wrote a work of tedious length describing all the heretical beliefs of his contemporaries. Among these he included various forms of Judaism, though it is important to remember that Judaism never officially came to be identified with heresy. This was fortunate for the survival of the Jews, for it meant that it was never possible just to forbid them to exist, in the manner in which later Roman and Byzantine Emperors treated those of their Christian subjects who failed to adjust their beliefs immediately to the imperial pattern. The effort to identify Judaism and heresy forms quite an interesting story, which continues right into the Middle Ages and the early Inquisition, and includes many of the more ridiculous apocryphal Gospels and Acts of Saints and Apostles.[9] To return to Epiphanius. He is supposed to have been of Palestinian origin, and converted at the age of sixteen. He included seven forms of Judaism in his work on heresies: Sadducees, Scribes, Pharisees, Hemerobaptists, Nazareans, Ossenes, and Herodians.[10] What he has to say of these sects is almost wholly without value. The Scribes, for example, admit four interpreters: "Moses, Akiba, Annanus or Judas, and the four sons of Assamoneus." The Ossenes are "spiritually disingenuous and intellectually ingenious," and the Herodians are "real Jews, being lazy and dishonest." The only value of the work of Epiphanius is that it exposes the depth of the ignorance of the Church of the nature and content of Jewish beliefs. For Epiphanius was regarded as the greatest authority on the subject.

This ignorance was partly due to the almost complete lack of Hebrew scholars. None of the Jews who became converts to Christianity during this period seem to have been men of eminence or learning; and the Church felt no need to know the content of Jewish contemporary literature. In fact, the only Church father who makes a parade of Hebrew learning is Jerome (c. 340–420) who lived in Palestine where there was still a considerable Jewish population. Even in his case it does not seem to have passed much beyond a knowledge of the Biblical language, which he found of value both for his translation of the Bible into Latin and for his arguments with Jews.

What is true of the Greek and Western Church fathers as a body is equally true of those who actually wrote disputations or polemics on Judaism and Jewish incredulity or, as it was called, perfidia. None of them knew Hebrew; none of them had anything but the vaguest ideas of Jewish belief. The Jew whom they introduce in many of these polemics is simply a dummy. Justin Martyr (c. 100–65), one of the fairest as well as earliest of these writers, makes his Jewish opponent describe the whole content of Judaism in these words: "to keep the Sabbath, to be circumcised, to observe months, to be washed if you touch anything prohibited by Moses or after sexual intercourse."[11]

But they not only showed no knowledge of contemporary Judaism; they gradually came to make a complete caricature of the Judaism and Jewish history which was known to them from the Old Testament. An anonymous tract against the Jews of the fourth or fifth century, and ascribed to Cyprian, thus summarises Jewish history:[12]

> *"Moses they cursed because he proclaimed Christ,*
> *Dathan they loved because he did not proclaim Him:*
> *Aaron they rejected because he offered the image of Christ,*
> *Abiron they set up because he opposed Him.*
> *David they hated because he sang of Christ,*
> *Saul they magnified because he did not speak of Him:*
> *Samuel they cast out because he spoke of Christ.*
> *Cham (Egypt?) they served because he said nothing of Christ:*
> *Jeremiah they stoned while he was hymning Christ,*
> *Ananias they loved while he was opposing Him:*
> *Isaiah they sawed asunder shouting His glories,*
> *Manasseh they glorified persecuting Him:*
> *John they slew revealing Christ,*
> *Zachariah they slaughtered loving Christ,*
> *Judas they loved betraying Him."*

It is not to be supposed that such an attitude led many Jews to embrace Christianity, and indeed there is very little evidence of conversions during this period. For the arguments which the Church used to prove the truth of her claims were such that any educated Jew would be able to answer. The Jews, in fact, did answer them, and though caution often compelled their answers to be oblique they had an effect, as we know not only from the emphasis in some of the special addresses prepared for catechumens warning them against Jewish arguments, but from the writings on general theological subjects of the Eastern fathers, members of whose congregations were bound to have Jewish acquaintances.

It was not argument, however, but legislation which came to be the Church's strongest weapon against the Synagogue. For in the fourth century the Empire accepted Christianity and the political influence of some of the great Church figures of the time was paramount. Even Theodosius the Great (*imp.* 379–95) feared to anger Ambrose, Bishop of Milan (340–97). While most of the legislation aimed at preventing Jews from coming to any prominent position in the official, commercial or social life of the Empire, other laws definitely excluded them from certain professions and occupations, and the combined effect of what was an attack on their citizenship and their legal equality with other citizens was a blow from which Jewry has not yet recovered. For it led to the long period of ghetto life, of political impotence and social ostracism which was only partially lifted by the emancipation of the nineteenth century. Even the internal affairs of the Jewish community were the subject of legislation. Their judicial autonomy and certain tax immunities were abolished, new synagogues were forbidden to be built, the circumcision of slaves became a crime, and even the conduct of service in synagogues came under the regulations of Justinian. If Christian legislation had little effect on converting Jews to Christianity, it explains why Jews have come to believe that Judaism is hostile to conversion to Judaism. For the very first law of the Roman Empire passed under Christian influence[13] on October 18th, 315, enacts that:

"We desire the Jews and their elders and patriarchs to be informed that if after the passage of this law anyone who flees from their gloomy sect to the worship of God is pursued by them with stones or any other molestation, as we know is at present happening, the offender shall immediately be consigned to the flames, with all those who have taken part in the offence. But if any person shall join himself to their evil sect, and give himself to their assemblies [*conciliabulis*, the slang word for "brothel"], he shall suffer the same punishment."

Theodosius II added the same penalty for the Jew responsible for the conversion.[14]

To put the matter into its true perspective it must be realised that the legislation against Jews formed part of a whole mass of legislation against divergence of belief. Though Jews were never formally identified with heretics, and by the standard of treatment of heretics might be considered favoured, yet the idea that Judaism should be a subject of legislation at all was accepted because men were already perverted by the idea that legislation should be brought into the field of personal belief. One of the most pernicious innovations of the Christian Emperors was the belief that only in a State with conformity on matters of faith could there be civil peace. It is not possible to defend this development in the Christian tradition by the argument that such ideas were universally held at this period of human development. They were not. Rabbinic Judaism was prepared to be exceedingly intolerant in matters of practice, but in many cases, including usually any question of belief, "punishment" was left to the Almighty. It would be said, for example, that those who held such and such a view would have no share in the life to come. The Roman was prepared to be brutal on matters of public order, but he was completely indifferent on matters of faith that did not disturb public order. Nor can the third source of Christian civilisation, Greece, be made responsible; the conception of philosophic uniformity enforced by law would scarcely even have qualified as a subject for a play by Aristophanes, so ridiculous would it have appeared. It is a Christian development, a short-cut solution to the problem created by the recognition of the extreme importance of right belief, and has been, and still is, wholly damnable in its effects, and without a single argument in its favour. It certainly *explains* why certain good and gentle Christian leaders may not have blenched at enforcing barbarous legislation against heretics or Jews, but it scarcely *excuses* one sin to say that it was a natural implication of another. It acted to increase the already fierce intolerance between the diverse Christian sects, since it presented men with the alternative of "kill or be killed." If they could not secure power over legislation from their enemies, their enemies would use that power to exterminate them.[15] The spectacle of mutual slaughter and mutilation between Christian sects became endemic in the religious life of the Byzantine Church in Asia, Syria and Palestine until all alike, orthodox or heretic, fell under the heel of Islam.

In such an environment it is not surprising that the laws of the fourth and fifth century, and the constant denunciations of the theologians, led at some times and in some places to local violence against Jews.[16] For there are laws insisting that Jews shall not be disturbed in the rights left to them, and that their synagogues are not to be pulled down. On the last point a quarrel between Theodosius the Great and Ambrose over the burning of a synagogue at Callinicum in Asia is most significant. The whole incident is graphically described by Ambrose himself in two letters to his sister.[17] The Christians of Callinicum, led by the bishop in person, had burnt down the Jewish synagogue. The Jews complained to the Governor, and the offenders were punished. The bishop was ordered to rebuild the synagogue at his own expense. This sentence was confirmed by the Emperor and came to the ears of Ambrose, who at once wrote a furious letter to his sovereign, telling him that he was forcing the bishop to become either an apostate or a martyr. He denied that the bishop had committed any crime, and added that if the Emperor disagreed, he might as well punish Ambrose himself, since only laziness had prevented him from burning down the synagogue in his cathedral city of Milan. Not content with such a letter, Ambrose publicly refused the Emperor communion until he had forced him, on the spot, to agree to cancel the Governor's sentence. In other words, the bishop interfered successfully to prevent the Emperor enforcing in favour of the Jews the actual laws of the Empire.

The writers of the Eastern Churches, and Eastern writers of the Empire, show somewhat more knowledge of Jewish life than their Western brothers, and this is natural for they were in closer contact with actual Jews. Aphrahat, known as the Persian sage (middle of fourth century) is one of the most interesting of these. In general, he writes with respect and without venom—for a fourth-century controversialist. He deals with circumcision, with the Sabbath and with various other matters, and shows some knowledge of what he writes about.[18] As time went on and the intellectual level of the literature declined, it actually becomes more possible to discover in Eastern disputations the main lines of the Jewish reply to Christian claims. For since the Jew in the dialogue was always to be converted ultimately by a miracle, the fact that he had won the intellectual argument would only enhance the miracle by which he finally admitted the superiority of Christianity. One of the most remarkable of this type is the *Dialogue of Gregentius, Archbishop of Tephren, with the Jew Herbanus*. Its date is of the seventh or eighth century. In the dispute Herbanus again and again convicts the archbishop of error in his method of interpreting the Old Testament, and may well be giving actual Jewish arguments.

The fact that Eastern Christians were accustomed to the presence of Jewish neighbours led to a new development at the time of the great iconoclastic controversy of the eighth century. The iconodules—the party who desired to retain the use of images in the churches—produced a series of stories whose point was the conversion of a Jew by an image, thereby showing that images possessed extraordinary power. The story which ultimately became Shakespeare's *Merchant of Venice* originated at this time in the tale of the debts of the Christian merchant, Theodore of Constantinople, and the loans of Abraham the Jew.[19] More usually the Jew attacks an image which bleeds and either leads to his conversion or at least betrays him to the Christians. Many of these stories travelled all through the Christian world and they are familiar in many monastic versions made during the Middle Ages in western Europe. The iconoclastic controversy is thus interesting as providing the first example of Jews being used as a scapegoat in a controversy which really had nothing to do with them.

For the story that the whole attack on images was due to a promise made to a Jewish fortune-teller by the Emperor Leo the Isaurian,[20] while he was still a simple shepherd, is as obviously mythical as the story that Jews stabbed sacred wafers or wrote the Protocols of the Elders of Zion.

Compared with the Christian material on the subject of the Jews, the amount of material which has survived from the Jewish side about the Christians is, at the beginning, both minute and relatively uninteresting. It is argued that one of the reasons for the codification of Jewish practice in the period of the Tannaim was to present a clearer and more united front to Christian propaganda than was possible with the multiplicity of sects and practices in the period before A.D. 70. But apart from the Malediction on the Nazarenes, and the letters to the synagogues refuting this new heresy and sent out about A.D. 100 (of which we possess no authentic text) there is no explicit statement dealing with the issue. During the second century the beginning of a rival story of the life of Jesus makes its appearance,[21] and it may be, as some have suggested, that its framework was deliberately taken over from the lost Gospel of the Hebrews used by the Judeo-Christians.[22] The *Sepher Toldoth Jeshu* (Book of the History of Jesus) probably gathered size and virulence as the centuries of Christian persecution proceeded, until it assumed its final form in the thirteenth century. But in its barest outline it was already known to Celsus, the third-century pagan opponent of Christianity.

In controversy Jews had always the advantage of knowledge of Hebrew, and their main line of argument was simply exposition of the actual meaning of the texts used by the Christians—a method which would have been likely to be very successful in preventing conversions of Jews, but which had little effect on the Church, since the Jewish expositions were made in Hebrew, and it would have been dangerous, indeed impossible, to translate them into Greek or Latin.

As to general relations during the pre-medieval period, the verdict must be that they were friendly, except when a particular act or individual stirred up controversy. Much imperial and canonical legislation is only explicable on this basis, and there is plenty of incidental information to confirm it. [23] In the same way it is true that during this period Jewish social and economic distribution was normal, except where legislation deflected its development. In the Middle Ages "usurer" often meant Jew. There is no occupational title in antiquity which has the same meaning.

The two significant facts with which the medieval period opens are that, with the disappearance of Roman Law, whittled down though it had been by the influence of the Church over legislation, the Jew had no political status of his own whatever; and that, as a result of nearly a thousand years of Christian preaching, the public was coming to believe any story, however absurd, about the conduct or beliefs of its Jewish contemporaries. Hence the rightlessness of medieval Jewry; hence the massacres of the first Crusade.

There is nothing in the early medieval situation which supports the theories which trace the whole of antisemitism either to zenophobia or to purely economic causes. Early medieval society was not so organised that conscious national thought was possible. It was in religion only, and not in any other field, that Jews could be regarded as abnormal. Likewise, there was no change or development in the economic structure of Jewry during the eleventh century which could explain the violence of the massacres of 1096, directed as they were in the first place against the oldest and most familiar Jewish settlements in western Europe. For some at least of the Rhineland Jewries dated from Roman times, possibly from the passage of the armies of Titus to the Rhineland frontier.

It is not possible to over-emphasise the psychological and social effects on Jewish consciousness of the rightlessness of the Middle Ages, and these effects are still with us. The words used by a fourteenth-century French Monarch [24] to describe the situation of the Jew might have been used by a Jewish organisation to describe the condition of most of the Jews of Europe in 1946:

"Jews have no country or place of their own in all Christendom where they can live and move and have their being, except by the purely voluntary permission and goodwill of the lord or lords under whom they wish to settle to dwell under them as their subjects, and who are willing to receive and accept them to this end."

Even in such countries as contemporary England, Jews have become conscious that their political rights are dependent, as those of non-Jews are not, on the absence of a political régime of a Nazi or Fascist type. And present circumstances do not allow them to regard the emergence of such a régime as an absolute impossibility. No English non-Jew would trouble to assert that he believes his political rights to be inviolable, and his relation to the soil of England sacrosanct; that English assimilationist Jews assert their belief in such rights is itself a distinction and an admission. As Pinsker says in *Auto-emancipation*, even when Jewish life is not regulated by special laws, it needs a special law to stipulate that this shall be so!

It is likewise impossible to overemphasise the importance of the fact that the ability of the common man to believe anything which is told him about the Jews derives ultimately from a millennium of Christian preaching throughout a period when there was no social or economic fact or moral or ethical standard of belief which distinguished him from his Jewish neighbours. It is wrong to identify the medieval situation either with Egyptian or Greco-Roman anti-Jewish feeling. For the essential difference is that the latter hostilities were based on views of actual Jewish conduct, or were part of the normal frictions of group-life; while the former were unrelated to any facts in the Jewish situation and derived solely from an imaginary portrait of "the Jews" drawn by the theologians. It is only as the Middle Ages progress, and the figure of the Jewish usurer becomes familiar, that the foundations of economic antisemitism are laid.

But before that could happen religious fanaticism, aided by ignorance and superstition, had made Jewish life a misery throughout the greater part of Europe. The sporadic nature of the physical attacks made upon them, and the edicts of banishment or repression issued against them, clearly mark the non-economic and non-political nature of the hatred in which they came to be held. They would be expelled by one prince and received by another, whose political situation and economic status were identical. In one diocese there would be constant harrying; in its neighbour peace. This intensification of hostility was due, in general terms, to the facts already described; the rightlessness of the Jews, their diversion to moneylending, and the use made by the clergy of the denunciations of the Old Testament. But the Middle Ages also added new charges of their own, not directly due to Biblical sources.

Earlier centuries had failed to identify the words "Jew" and "heretic." The Middle Ages identified the words "Jew" and "devil." Joshua Trachtenberg, in his monograph on the subject, writes:[25]

"The most vivid impression to be gained from a reading of medieval allusions to the Jew is of a hatred so vast and abysmal, so intense, that it leaves one gasping for comprehension. The unending piling up of vile epithets, and accusations and curses, the consistent representation of the Jew as the epitome of everything evil and abominable, for whom in particular the unbounded scorn and contumely of the Christian world were reserved, must convince the most casual student that we are dealing here with a fanaticism altogether subjective and non-rational."

It is quite impossible to accept the idea that feelings which merit such a description could arise from dislike of a usurer! The Jew as devil, the Jew whose badge was a scorpion, the symbol of falsity,[26] owes his origin to religion, not to economics.

Equally religious in origin, and even more devastating in effect, was the charge that Judaism ordained the practice of ritual murder on the bodies of Christians in order to secure blood for mixing with the unleavened bread used at Passover. The first case of which we have evidence is that of William of Norwich in 1144,[27] and it is worth noting that it took more than six years before the boy came to be regarded as a martyr and a saint, victim of a ritual act of the Jewish community.

Not content with creating the ritual murder legend, medieval religion produced an interesting variant of the use, in the iconoclastic controversy, of the Jews as a scape-goat. In the thirteenth century arose a dispute concerning certain doctrines of the Mass, and the practice of communi-cating the laity with the consecrated wafer (or Host) only, and not with the chalice (or wine). At this time appeared stories that the Jews stole the sacred wafer from the churches and vented their hatred on the Founder of Christianity by stabbing it. The result of the act was—so rumour spread— that the wafer bled. Just as the importance of images was proved by their ability to convert Jews five hundred years earlier, so now it was conveniently shown to the laity that they were receiving both the body and blood of their Redeemer by the fact that when a Jew stabbed the conse-crated wafer, blood came out.

So far as the many writings recording real or imaginary disputations with Jews during the Middle Ages are con-cerned, there is nothing substantial to be added to what has already been recorded, save in the single case of Spain. The earliest Spanish document is that of the converted Jew, Samuel of Morocco, of the year 1072. I need not go here into the claim of Steinschneider that it is in fact a Dominican forgery of the fourteenth century, but I share the view of Lukyn Williams that it is more likely to be genuine.[28] This small work is remarkable for one point. Though there is nothing of special originality in its argument, it is almost the only work in a mass of literature which would fill thousands of pages dealing with the conversion of the Jews, in which there are no sneers, no gibes, no threats, but a tone throughout of genuine friendliness.

The Spanish works are remarkable, indeed unique, for one reason. They are almost entirely written by men with an

intimate knowledge of Hebrew, and a considerable acquaint-
ance with rabbinic and Talmudic literature. The reason is
that they were either converts from Judaism, or had been
trained in the special schools established in the thirteenth
century by the Dominicans for preparing missionaries to the
Jews and Moslems in the languages and literature of their
prospective converts.

The first of the writings in this class is the *Dialogue of Peter
the Christian convert with Moses the Jew*. Its author is Peter
Alphonsi (1062–1100) a convert of Huesca in Aragon. It
is a long work and deals extensively with all contemporary
philosophies, and with Islam as well as Judaism. But its
main Jewish interest lies in its violent attack on the Haggadic
element of the Talmud, with which Peter was naturally
familiar. He regards the anthropomorphism of the Haggadoth as trivial, ridiculous, and improper; and there is, no
doubt, truth in the attack, once the Haggadah is approached
without any knowledge of the environment in which it was
composed, or familiarity with the imagery and imagination
of oriental works. Peter, had he been more familiar with
oriental Christian, especially monastic, literature, would
have found almost as much to shock him; and the Book of
Revelation itself contains enough anthropomorphisms about
the Son to show its kinship with Talmudic imagination.

At the beginning of the thirteenth century there was born
at Montpellier a Jew, who is known to us as Paulus
Christiani (*d.* 1274). He became a Dominican, and con-
ducted missions among the Jews of the South of France.
Being regarded as their chief exponent, he was chosen by his
Order to conduct the Christian side in the disputation
which was arranged in 1263 at Barcelona, by order of
James I of Aragon. His opponent was the famous Rabbi
Nachmanides. Two accounts of the disputation survive, one
drawn up by the Dominicans, one by Nachmanides. Each
naturally claims the victory. But so fair a Christian scholar
as Lukyn Williams, after examining both, pronounces in
favour of the text and verdict of Nachmanides.[29] In any
case, the Dominicans were sufficiently hostile to him for it

to be deemed wise that he should leave the country, and he became one of the famous Jewish "exiles" of the Middle Ages from the Galuth to Eretz Israel. There are two points of interest in the record of the disputation. On the Jewish side, Nachmanides, for the first time in our recorded literature, tries to make Paulus see that the Messiah in Jewish thought does not occupy the place occupied by Jesus as Messiah in that of Christians. In other words, Judaism is a *different kind of religion from Christianity*, and its central interest is not salvation and redemption, for which a Messiah, in the Christian interpretation of His office, would occupy the centre of the picture. The other point is one made by Paulus, and both reflects and foreshadows interesting developments. The idea had been a constant theme of apocryphal Gospels and Acts, and is frequently met with in oriental disputations (such as the *Doctrina Jacobi*, or the story of *Theodosius and Philip*),[30] that in their hearts the Jews knew that Christianity was true. The effort to identify Judaism and heresy rested on this basis. Paulus claims of the Haggadoth that they reveal in innumerable ways that the Jews knew that the Messiah would be just like Jesus, though never explicitly admitting the identification. In the sixteenth century Christians believed that the doctrine of the Trinity was to be found in the Qabbala.

A greater contemporary of Paulus was Raymond Martin (*c.* 1225–85), a Christian by birth, who studied at the school established by the Dominicans, and was appointed censor of confiscated Hebrew books in Aragon. In 1278 he published the most important of all the works of the Spanish school, the *Pugio Fidei* (Dagger of the Faith). This is, in effect, an immense encyclopædia containing not only all the scriptural texts usually adduced to prove to Jews the truth of the Christian religion, but vast numbers of texts from Talmudic and other rabbinic literature which, according to Martin, were susceptible of a Christian interpretation. It had of course always been implicit, if not explicit, in Christian teaching that the Hebrews of the Old Testament were Trinitarians who looked to Jesus as Messiah. Hence the

EJC

Church's confident use of the Old Testament scriptures to prove her points. With Martin this belief is carried through as consistently into the Talmudic period. Raymond Martin's work was used extensively by later writers—usually without acknowledgment—and especially by another convert, Hieronymus de Sancta Fide (*fl. c.* 1400), who, in his *De Judaicis Erroribus ex Talmud,* provides also a storehouse of all the sayings and stories which Christian censors found ridiculous, obscene or blasphemous in Jewish rabbinical writings. It is interesting that Hieronymus is the chief medieval source quoted by Eisenmenger, author of the main storehouse of modern religious antisemitism.

A much greater and more original writer was Paul of Burgos (1358–1435), born Solomon ha-Levi, and dying Archbishop of the city in which he was born. Like his Spanish predecessors he was a competent Jewish scholar, and the tone in which he addresses his former coreligionists in his *Scrutinium Scripturarum* is, for the period, moderate and considerate. Had the Christian administration which he upheld been equally considerate, Jewry would have been spared much suffering. But the background of his writings is a persecution which, partly by the very fact that so many converted Jews were among the persecutors, was more far-reaching and deadly than any suffered by the Jews during the Middle Ages. Vincent Ferrer (1350–1419), whose companion and inspiration was Hieronymus de Sancta Fide, was its leader and claimed thousands of converts. But like their successors in the days of the Spanish Inquisition, they were mostly converts from fear, not from conviction.

The detail to be found in the works of the Spanish authors is due to their access, whether as Jews or censors, to all available Hebrew literature. The most durable effect of their activity was not, however, the denunciations of Talmudic Judaism which they produced, but the succession of officials which they provided for the medieval Inquisition's censorship of Hebrew books. It is well known that only one medieval copy of the Talmud survived in 1939. It was at Munich, and whether it still exists I do not know. But the mere fact that it is the only survival, together with the extreme rarity of medieval Hebrew manuscripts in general—apart from copies of the Psalms, most of which were made for Christians, and many of which were written by Christians—testifies to the efficiency with which the medieval Church destroyed the centres of Jewish learning in western Europe. In the fourth decade of the thirteenth century, both in France and in Spain, all available Jewish books were suddenly seized while the Jews were at synagogue. The result in Paris alone was the burning of twenty-four cart-loads,[31] and even if this be an exaggeration, or the cartloads very small, yet the loss was an irreparable one. The decline in Jewish scholarship and vitality which becomes marked as the Middle Ages draw to their close was not due so much to internal decay and loss of creative thought as to this external and physical destruction of Jewish centres of learning, and to the conservatism and narrowness which arise in all religions when persecution becomes intolerable and experiment a mortal danger.

There is, however, a considerable body of Jewish polemic and apologetic dating from the Middle Ages. It has its origin earlier in the almost casual references to some Christian interpretation or doctrine in a work of Jewish interest which was not expected to be read by Christians. The starting point was usually some question of Biblical exegesis, since the Christians attempted to prove so much from their use of the Old Testament, and were so woefully ignorant of its Hebrew text that they made mistakes which were not difficult for a Jewish scholar to point out. Hence arose the Christian charge that these Jewish refutations were based on the deliberate alteration of the text of the Bible since Jerome's Latin translation of the fifth century (the Vulgate). Fragments of a work of a tenth-century Jewish philosopher of Babylon, Al-Mukamis, have survived in which he argued, as many of his successors will do, that Christian monotheism is less pure than Jewish. His greater contemporary, the philosopher Saadia, Gaon of the rabbinical school at Sura in Babylonia (892–942), also dealt with various Christian doctrines in his work, *The Book of the Articles of Faith and Doctrines of Dogma*, dealing especially with theories of the nature of Jesus and the abrogation of Torah. He showed considerable knowledge of Eastern Christianity in his treatment. Jehudah Ha-Levi (1085–1145) and Maimonides (1135–1204) also treated of similar subjects; and the most famous work of Ha-Levi is the *Kuzari*, a three-cornered discussion between a Jew, a Christian and a Moslem.

The earliest known work dealing wholly with polemic against the Christian faith is that of the grammarian and Biblical commentator, Joseph Kimchi from Narbonne (1160–1235), whose *Book of the Covenant* adopts the familiar Christian form of a dialogue between a Jew and a Min (or heretic), the name by which Christians are usually designated in the Talmud. Like others of the same class, it deals largely with the use of Old Testament quotations, but also covers such questions as original sin and redemption. Such works were soon followed by notes of actual disputations, since from the thirteenth century onwards the Church not infrequently compelled famous rabbis to sustain public arguments with leading theologians. There is the discussion between Rabbi Jechiel of Paris and the converted Jew Nicholas Donin, and the more famous Spanish disputation, already referred to, between Paulus Christiani and Nachmanides. One important purpose in the circulation of these works among the Jewish community was to counter the possible effect of the conversional sermons which Jews were increasingly compelled to attend, sometimes in their own synagogues, sometimes in Christian churches in or near their ghettoes. These sermons were ordered by Pope Nicholas III in a Bull of 1278,[32] directed to the Dominicans of Lombardy, but they had already been introduced in various countries.

It was apparently not until the end of the fourteenth century that the Church became fully aware of the existence of this literature, and naturally set out to reply to it and to suppress it. Several of the works of this time have, however, survived,

and give an excellent idea of the line of Jewish attack and
defence. Two of the most important have their origin in
the violent persecution which befel the Jews of Spain in 1391,
under the influence of Vincent Ferrer. In this persecution
a Catalonian Jew, Profiat Duran (c. 1350 to c. 1400), tutor
in the house of the leading scholar and statesman of Spanish
Jewry, Chasdai Crescas (c. 1340–1412), was forcibly baptised
together with a friend of his. They planned to flee from the
country to Palestine, there to return to Judaism. Duran
set out, but his friend decided at the last minute to retain
his new faith. In disgust, Duran wrote him a satirical letter,
Be not like your Ancestors, which, on the surface, counselled
him to remain in the Christian faith and not to return
to the faith of his fathers. The letter came into the hands
of the clergy, who took it seriously, and circulated it widely,[33]
until it began to dawn on them that it was a satire on
Christianity and that in each argument logic and common
sense was to be found in the faith ascribed to the friend's
fathers, i.e. Judaism. Duran followed up the letter with a
longer work, written at the request of Crescas, entitled *The
Shame of the Gentiles*. In this work he examined Christianity
systematically, showing an adequate knowledge of the New
Testament and of Christian doctrine. An interesting point
which he made is that the Gospels show that Jesus had no
intention of founding a new religion. This book became a
standard textbook used by other Jewish scholars, including
his employer, Chasdai Crescas, who had suffered even more
seriously in the troubles of 1391, losing one of his sons as a
martyr to his faith. At the request of some Spanish Christian
friends, Crescas, using the material Duran had prepared for
him, wrote in Spanish a profound philosophic work entitled
Refutation of the Cardinal Principles of Christianity, in which
he contrasted the philosophic simplicity of Judaism with the
contradictions and complications of Christian doctrine.

Almost simultaneously with these Spanish polemists, a
Jew who lived most of his life in Prague, Yom Tob Lipmann
Mülhausen (c. 1380–1459), was moved by similar experi-
ences to a similar activity. He was denounced by a convert,

Peter, as having written things insulting to Christianity. In the persecution which followed, over seventy Jews lost their lives, but Rabbi Lippmann survived. Round about 1400 he produced a book entitled *The Book of Victory* (*Sepher Ha-Nizachon*) which became the best known of all these works, and provoked a Christian reply from Stephen Bodeker, Bishop of Brandenburg, as early as 1459. The work is acute and even abusive, but of less philosophic worth than that of the Spaniards. His method of writing lent itself less to philosophy, as the work consists of comments on over three hundred verses of the Bible, taken in order. The final work of this group also came from eastern Europe, from one of the most famous scholars of the Jewish sect of Karaites, Isaac of Troki (1533–94). Isaac was well versed in contemporary Christian literature, and familiar with many of the Christian sects of the period, whose members found a refuge in the liberal Poland of the great renaissance kings, Sigismund II (*r.* 1548–72) and Stephen Batory (*r.* 1576–86). The great work of Isaac is entitled *The Strengthening of the Faith* (*Chissuk Emunah*), and the larger part of it is an apologetic for Judaism against Christian attacks upon it. In the second half he turns to the attack, and accuses the Christians, not only of contradictions and absurdities in their doctrines, but also of not being loyal to them. Though written when printing presses were in full swing in Poland, the work was circulated in manuscript for fear of the censor. It came into the hands of Christians in the seventeenth century and has produced a considerable literature of reply, which has continued down to this day. The existence of the censorship caused Jewish authors to be slow to take advantage of printing for their apologetic, and the first book printed in a European vernacular is *Der Jüdische Theriac* (*Jewish Medicine*) by Zalman Ofenhausen, published in 1615 as a reply to a scurrilous attack by a convert, Samuel Brenz, published under the pseudonym of F. v. Ittingen—*Der Jüdische Schlangenbalg* (*The Jewish Snakeskin*).

We cannot, however, leave the Middle Ages without reference to the fact that medieval Christian princes embodied their attitude to Jewry in more than verbal denunciation. The rightlessness in which Jewry was abandoned when the traditions of Roman law finally gave way before Christian and feudal substitutes deprived the Jews of any possible appeal, save the limited and humiliating power of bribery, against injustice, expulsion or even death. Jews were as much the personal property of a medieval prince as his gloves or his hounds; and the same, of course, applied to their possessions. The usury which they were obliged to practise for the benefit of their masters, who used them as a sponge to soak up the wealth of their subjects, humbled their pride, destroyed their self-respect, and increased their insecurity, until finally they became as outcast and even deformed as their most ardent enemies could wish.

Nor was the Church behindhand in ensuring their humiliation. The record of the Papacy itself is good in so far as mob violence or attempts at conversion by force are concerned; and successive Popes confirmed the denial of the charge of ritual murder.[34] But the Papacy was naturally the authority primarily responsible for enforcing on the Jews a status which the Church Fathers had deduced, as appropriate to a deicide nation, from their interpretation of the New Testament. The Jewish badge, segregation and the ghetto, the conversional sermon, the destruction of Jewish books, all owe their origin to or were confirmed by Papal policy.[35] As to the clergy, when they were themselves territorial princes, their policy was indistinguishable from that of the secular princes; and the local clergy shared the views of the populace, and often created their superstitions and directed their violence. From the clergy who led the massacres in the Rhineland during the First Crusade in 1096 to Vincent Ferrer in Spain at the end of the fourteenth century, there is scarcely any example of mob violence in which we do not find clerics involved.

The introduction of printing immensely increased the knowledge which each religion might have acquired of the other. Eisenmenger in 1700 lists over one hundred and fifty printed Hebrew books with which he was familiar—or said he was—and which he used in the preparation of his work. Books to protect Christians from Jewish influence, books to convert the Jews, poured out from the presses of Europe. The Talmud itself was printed, though fairly heavily censored by the Inquisition's officers. But, at the same time, this activity merely produced more in quantity of material whose quality differed in nothing from that of the Middle Ages. A new approach came only slowly and from a few authors. In this field Reuchlin's counsel on whether Jewish books should be destroyed, published in 1511 under the pleasant title of *Augenspiegel (Spectacles)*, an answer to Pfefferkorn's *Judenspiegel*, occupies an honoured place. He first defended the Talmud, and recommended that only two Hebrew works should be destroyed, the *Sepher Ha-Nizachon (The Book of Victory)* of R. Lipmann Mülhausen of Prague, and the *Sepher Toldoth Jeshu*.

The breakdown of the medieval unity of Christendom had no immediate effects on relations with Jews. As we shall see in the next chapter, the Reformers and the new Churches shared the opinions of the old in such matters, and works were printed by Catholic and Protestant alike, following the old lines. Only two of these need mention, both produced by scholars of German origin, the former a Roman Catholic and the latter a Protestant. In 1681 John Christopher Wagenseil, Professor at Altdorf, dedicated to the Princes, Magistrates, Theologians and People of Christendom his collection of *The Fiery Darts of Satan (Tela Ignea Sathani)*, the secret writings of the Jews against Christianity. Here he collected, commented and translated into Latin the *Acrostic* ascribed erroneously to R. Lipmann, a *Sepher Ha-Nizachon*, the disputations of R. Jechiel with Nicholas Donin, and of Paulus Christiani with Nachmanides, the *Chissuk Emunah (Strengthening of Faith)* of R. Isaac of Troki, and the *Sepher Toldoth Jeshu*. Nineteen years later John Andrew Eisenmenger of Heidelberg produced what was to become the textbook of all modern attacks on the Talmud—*Judaism Revealed (Entdecktes Judenthum)*. The oriental exaggeration of much Haggadic fancy appeared even more fantastic in the light of the rationalism of seventeenth-century Protestantism, and Eisenmenger's work was drawn on from every motive, serious or anecdotic. A translation of a good deal of it appeared in English under the title *Traditions of the Jews*, by J. P. Stehelin, about thirty years later.

The invention of printing led also to new forms of popular abuse of the Jews and to the production of many woodcuts and broadsheets with more or less obscene drawings supposed to represent Jewish life.[36] Ritual murder, Jews suckling a sow, and fantastic pictures of the Jewish expectation of the Messiah formed the most popular stock-in-trade of the vendors of such objects.

Emancipation brought a new type of literature into existence in that Jews, for the first time, openly defended themselves, and made public reply to the Christian attacks on their religion. With the works which resulted I shall deal in the next chapter, but they mark the distinction between medieval and modern antisemitism. To the attacks of Chrysostom or of Paulus Christiani, no open reply was possible. To those of Stöcker or Rohling, Jews answered freely.

While there was never a period in which no anti-Jewish literature appeared, there was a very definite increase in its output towards the middle of the nineteenth century; and that century also witnessed the appearance of a new centre from which such literature emanated—Tsarist Russia. In general, it must be said of modern antisemitism that its strength lies in the political and economic rather than the religious field. Yet neither Protestant nor Roman Catholic, nor Eastern Orthodox Churches, can dissociate themselves from considerable responsibility both for the rekindling of the flames of Jew-hatred and for aiding in the dissemination of the poison of antisemitism. At the very beginning of modern political antisemitism in the 1880's, the Lutheran Court Chaplain, Adolf Stöcker, was leading the German antisemitic movement from Berlin, while a young German Roman Catholic priest, Augustus Rohling, was distributing anti-Jewish propaganda from his press and pulpit in the

Rhineland. Rohling later was given a professorship at the, then Austrian, University of Prague, where he specialised in the encouragement of every libel on the Talmud and in the repetition of accusations of ritual murder. In the last decade of the nineteenth century the circles of political Roman Catholicism in France were heavily compromised in the *Affaire Dreyfus*. Meanwhile, in the territory of the Orthodox Churches matters were no better. In the Balkan countries the blood accusation thrived, not without assistance from Orthodox clergy. In Russia the Orthodox Church was equally gravely guilty, in addition to conniving at the forced baptism of military recruits and at the general anti-Jewish policy of the Tsarist bureaucracy. The most fanatical of the anti-Jewish politicians, as well as the most influential adviser of the governments of Alexander III and Nicholas II, was Constantin Petrovich Pobiedonostsev (1827–1907), Procurator (i.e. President) of the Holy Synod of the Orthodox Church. Even in the last twenty-five years none of the Churches can show an absolutely clear record. Some of the Protestant theological colleges in Germany were hotbeds of National-Socialism even before Hitler came to power. Of the Roman Catholics it is enough to mention Father Coughlin in the United States, and of the Orthodox, Professor Cuza at the University of Jassy in Rumania, neither of whom was disowned by his Church until it was clear that the harm he was doing to its reputation was greater than the success with which he fomented antisemitism. It must be added also that some modern Christian writings on the subject have developed an unpleasant new technique of conveying innuendoes and malicious insinuations under the guise of objective scholarship and even friendly advice. I can think of a number of such works, written by both Roman Catholics and Protestants, which only the strange character of the law of libel, which declares that the greater the truth the greater the libel, obliges me not to quote.

Immense though the output of modern antisemitism has been, there is really nothing new in the works of such men as Canon Rohling. He has merely dug ignorantly in the vast quarry provided for him by Eisenmenger, and his followers have done the same. There is, in fact, only one surprising element in modern religious antisemitism, and that is not a new one. It is the success with which in central and eastern Europe it has proved possible to resurrect among both Roman Catholics and Eastern Orthodox Christians the legend of ritual murder. There are almost more examples of the accusation in the years between 1880 and 1945 than in the whole of the Middle Ages, and the legend was revived because it was still of great value to nineteenth-century political antisemitism to be able to rely on an unbroken tradition of religious hostility, which could be exploited for political ends.

The subject matter for this chapter has inevitably been a depressing one. Christianity is essentially a missionary religion. That it should have striven through the centuries to convert Jews to its faith is to be expected. That such an object should have been accompanied by so much violence, abuse and misrepresentation is humiliating for anyone who takes its principles seriously.

CHAPTER FIVE

THE REDISCOVERY THAT JEWS ARE A LIVING PEOPLE AND JUDAISM A LIVING RELIGION.

THE LAST CHAPTER DEALT with Judaism considered as a religion which had ceased to possess the truth, to its own final condemnation; and with the Jews considered as a people who had committed the unique sin of deicide and, having voluntarily called down on their own heads through all generations the penalities of such a sin, were justly suffering the divine vengeance. For it was on the basis of these two assumptions that the Christian view of both Judaism and the lot of the Jewish people was shaped through the many centuries during which the Church, whose power extended over the rulers of both thought and action, held the Jews in the hollow of her hand. And it has to be admitted that, with such linguistic palliatives as a more squeamish age necessitates, this traditional view of Judaism and of the Jewish people is still very commonly found throughout Christendom.

Those prepared to revise the traditional attitude are, therefore, still a "minority movement." We must follow odd threads through nearly two thousand years of European history, threads which are at all times tenuous and slender, and sometimes vanish entirely. Even to-day the idea that Judaism is to be considered as a normal living religion and the Jews as a normal living people nowhere dominates the thoughts of politicians or of churchmen, except perhaps in enlightened circles in Britain or the U.S.A.

In the last chapter it was necessary to keep rather rigorously to the religious aspect of the subject. This was partly because the field to cover was so large. But it was dictated even more by the conviction that religion lies at the root of antisemitism and that, apart from religious influences, the economic and political manifestations of that scourge, which now undoubtedly dominate the situation, would never have had so fertile a soil in which to grow. The present subject, however, is inevitably concerned also with the work of historians and politicians, with the progress of historical scholarship and with the effects of the emancipation of the Jews in the nineteenth century. For although this is a secularist age, it is one in which Judaism and the Jewish people are still—if I may coin the phrase—inseparably disunited. We are confronted with Jewish groups which regard it as a social or political necessity to proclaim themselves members of a religion; with other groups who regard it as a religious necessity to proclaim themselves as a people; and with yet others who, believing themselves to be saturated with the secularist spirit of the age, proclaim their right to inherit and transmit a culture or civilisation whose very existence is based on religion. The one feature which all have in common is the desire to escape from a régime of abnormality into what they, from their different standpoints, regard as a normal existence. Psychologically, and in terms of the desire for self-respect, the movements are identical. Their mutual conflicts, bitter though they are, are the product of the history which all alike share, and of the background described in the last chapter.

Since the beginning of Christianity there has been only one brief period in which there existed orthodox Christians who yet understood and shared the basic conceptions of Judaism. This was the original Judeo-Christian Church, and the period in which it was allowed to consider itself orthodox was short. The habit of the Church of destroying the documents of those she judged heretics prevents us from having any close knowledge of the tenets of these Judeo-Christians as they developed after the Apostolic Age. Yet so far as we know, it was their belief in the continuing validity of Torah, rather than any lack of belief in Jesus, which led to their rejection. But rejected they were, and the gap in understanding which they have left has not yet been filled.

In the subsequent period various movements within Christendom have been condemned as Judaising. Yet actually they never touched more than the fringe of Judaism. They adopted some Jewish observance, the Sabbath, distinction of meats, dislike of images, or even a unitarian form of theology. But they never approached the understanding of Judaism as a way of life based on Torah.

The same in general is true of the Christian Hebraists who are to be found among the theologians of almost every period. They sought a knowledge of Hebrew in order that it might aid them in their Christian interpretation of the Scriptures, not in order to understand Judaism. Those who, like the Spanish converts, had known Judaism themselves and were familiar with its practices, were its most prejudiced interpreters. The most remarkable medieval attempt to present it fairly comes not from a convert, but from a Christian-born Hebraist, Raymund Lull (1266–1315) who, in *The Gentile and the Three Wise Men*, described a romantic meeting of a pagan with a Christian, a Moslem and a Jew, with a real attempt to give a fair account of each religion.

The beginnings of a real change, however, came only with the Renaissance, and among a few of the more free-thinking scholars of that period. To the work of Reuchlin in defending the Talmud against the censorship reference has already been made. One or two of his contemporaries began to study Judaism for the purpose of discovering what was contained in its tenets, rather than of exposing what was erroneous in its beliefs. The transition is provided by the sudden passion for the Qabbala among such men as Reuchlin himself and Pico di Mirandola, a transition only, because much of their interest was aroused by their belief that in its mystical theology was a clear expression of the Christian doctrine of the Trinity. But in such a man as Jean Bodin (1530–96) it goes deeper. He studied Jewish religion and philosophy with no other apparent motive than to find out if they were true, and from various standpoints he set Jewish belief and interpretation of the universe higher than that of either Roman Catholics or Protestants. He found in the law of

Moses the perfect "natural" religion, and he considered rabbinic Judaism the proper interpretation of the religion of the prophets. The Jewish authors whom he cited range from the Mishna to the medieval philosophers.[1]

Yet such men were still but isolated episodes. The leaders of the Renaissance were more interested in the Greek and Roman than in the Judaic aspects of antiquity; and their reforming contemporaries in the religious field saw no reason to reverse the tradition of condemnation and contempt which they had inherited from their predecessors' interpretations of Paul and the evangelists. It appeared at first as though Martin Luther (1483–1546) might do something to effect a change. In his early days he was sympathetic towards the Jews; but it soon became clear that this was due to no fresh estimate of the nature of Judaism, but to the belief that they would more easily be persuaded to accept Christianity in the purified version which he offered them than in the medieval doctrine of the Catholic Church which he condemned. When he discovered that they were no more interested in the one than in the other, he turned on them with a vulgarity of abuse which exceeded that of all but the most infamous of his predecessors.[2] Though Luther's indifference to the political aspects of religion, as well as his passion for the extreme forms of the Pauline distinction between faith and works, might explain why there seemed to him to be nothing of spiritual interest in Judaism, it is more surprising that John Calvin (1509–64), with his determination to establish an ordered polity under strict religious control, should not have penetrated more deeply into the understanding of the significance of Sinai. Yet in the *Institutes*, in which he describes in detail his Christian society, there is no attempt to model it upon that of Moses, nor, indeed, any different attitude towards "the Law" than is to be found in traditional Christian writings.

It was not, however, Calvin, but Zwingli who was regarded as the most "Judaising" of the Reformers, and he was certainly the more eminent Hebraist, and more profoundly saturated with Old Testament feeling. In the

aristocratic Christian polity which he wished to establish, he
desired to introduce many individual Mosaic laws; and
considered that he was thereby modelling his society as
much on the Mosaic as the Christological foundation; for
he regarded the two Testaments as one, and the Christians
as heirs to both. But his use of the Old Testament could
only be called—though the phrase would have horrified him
—a mild form of Sadducaism, for it was only the written
Torah which he respected, and he saw no value in its
Jewish interpreters.

If the reformers themselves were little interested in
Judaism, yet the Reformation led to an immense revival
of the serious study of Hebrew, and the sixteenth and
seventeenth centuries saw chairs of Hebrew established in
all the leading universities in Protestant countries. This
interest in Hebrew arose naturally out of the substitution
of the Bible for the Church as the ultimate authority in all
religious questions. On such a basis it became exceedingly
important to deepen and widen the scope of Biblical study;
and this was quickly recognised to be impossible without a
profound knowledge of Hebrew which, needed originally
for purely Biblical studies, spread by way of interest in Jewish
Biblical commentators to an interest in the rabbinical
treatment of the Mosaic Law and so to the Talmud and to
rabbinic literature in general.

Among the scholars thus made familiar with the later
developments of Judaism three distinct views are to be
discovered. There were many who, objective and even
apparently sympathetic in their descriptions of detail,
yet continued to dismiss Judaism as a whole with the
traditional finality and contempt; others were nearer to the
"pure" scholarship of modern times, seeking only facts and
not concerned with such matters as their theological implications; while a very few were led by their studies to a new
sympathy with Judaism. The outstanding example of the
first attitude is the family of Buxtorf at Basle. The first to
make his name in this field was John Buxtorf (1564–1629),
whose *Synagoga Judaica*, originally produced in German in

1603, was constantly reproduced in authorised or unauthor- ised editions throughout the seventeenth and eighteenth centuries. The Buxtorfs formed a dynasty of Professors of Hebrew at Basle for over a century (John Buxtorf, great- grandson of the author of *Synagoga Judaica*, died in 1732), and their personal relations with Jews seem often to have been friendly; John Buxtorf the Elder, for example, incurred a fine of fl.100 for attending the circumcision of the child of a Jewish friend. Their scholarship was profound and usually objective, and yet they found in Judaism nothing which merited anything but the utmost contempt, which they expressed continuously in the most opprobious lan- guage. At the beginning of many editions of the *Synagoga* is to be found printed in large type one of Luther's more rancorous and offensive utterances, in which he affirms that the Jews would crucify ten Messiahs and God Himself, together with all the angels and the whole creation, and submit themselves to a thousand pains of the damned, rather than share their Messiah and their promises with the Goim. And at the end Buxtorf says:

"From all these points the Christian reader will see and understand readily enough that Judaism and the whole religion of the Jews is squarely based, not on Moses, but on mendacity, on false and futile traditions and on the fables of rabbis and charlatans. Christians must no longer say that Jews cling tightly to the law of Moses, but, with the prophet Jeremiah, that they have learned a lie and will not be turned from it."[3]

John Lightfoot (1602–75), the great Cambridge Talmud- ist, speaks in identical vein:[4]

"Both the Law and this (say they) God gave to Moses, the Law by day, and by writing, and this by night and by word of mouth. . . . And thus like fame in Vergil *crevit eundo*, like a snowball it grew bigger with going. Thus do they father their fooleries upon Moses, and Elders, and Prophets, who, (good men), never thought of such fancies. . . . Against this their tradition, Our Saviour makes part of His Sermon on the Mount, Matthew 5. But he touched the Jews freehold, when he touched their Talmud, for greater treasure in their conceits they had none: like Cleopatra in Plutarch, making much of the viper that destroyed them."

In another passage Lightfoot deals with the possibility of the Jews' conversion, and writes in tones which rival those of Luther:[5]

"I see not how we can look upon the conversion of the Jews under a lower notion than the conversion of a brood of *Antichrist*. Therefore can I no more look for the general calling of them, than I look for the general call of the *Antichrist*-ian group of Rome. We see indeed by happy experience that several Nations have fallen off from the Roman *Antichrist*, as the Protestant countries that are at this day: but *Antichrist* is yet in being and strong, and his end will be, not by conversion, but perdition."

While the views of men like Buxtorf, Lightfoot or Wagenseil were certainly the views of the majority of Christian scholars, there appear from the end of the sixteenth century a few who had simply a dispassionate interest in seeking the facts. One such was Peter van der Kuhn (Petrus Cunæus, 1586–1638), Professor of Jurisprudence at Leyden, and author of a work—*De Republica Hebraeorum*—in which he showed his preference for the Mosaic economy to that of the classical world, and freely quotes from rabbinic sources. A second lawyer and Dutchman who shared his point of view was the great international lawyer, Hugo Grotius (1583–1645), who exchanged many letters on rabbinical points with Manasseh ben Israel, the Dutch Jew who negotiated with Cromwell for the return of the Jews to England. A third lawyer may be added to their company, the Englishman John Selden (1584–1654), whose study of Jewish courts and legal procedure (*De Synedriis et Praefecturis Juridicis veterum Ebraeorum*) makes extensive and approving use of rabbinical commentaries and rabbinical developments of the Jewish legal system.

The most remarkable scholar of the third school of thought was William Surenhuis (Gulielmus Surenhusius, *c.* 1650–1710). He was Professor at Amsterdam, and in 1698 he began to publish the first Latin translation of the Mishnah, making use of the work of many different scholars for different tractates. In his Introduction he speaks with an extraordinary warmth of the value of the work of the Patriarch Judah Ha-Nasi, author of the Mishnah, going so far as to say that, after the terrible signs of God's wrath in the destruction of Jerusalem and the disasters which accompanied it,[6] "the sun appeared again behind the clouds. And when the wrath of God against the people of Israel had somewhat abated" He sent them Judah to continue the work of religious upbuilding. At another point he lauds the character of the Mishnah, and adds that "if the reader has a desire to abuse the Jews, he may do so in his own time and place, in so far as his Christian love permits him to do it, but he must never confuse matters of ritual with matters of faith," i.e. he must not pretend that because the Jews had a great concern with details of ritual this means that they were lacking in faith. He makes this point even more strongly in his inaugural dissertation as Professor in 1704—*Dissertatio de natura Pandectarum Hebraicarum*—in which he launches into a violent denunciation of the whole tribe of Buxtorfs and their followers and says of them:[7] "the true nature of the Talmud has never been understood by them. . . . O what incredible ignorance of Hebrew Law (they show), what monstrous discourses, what perverse thoughts."

Though the output on the Roman Catholic side was not comparable in originality, and it was indeed more difficult for them to approach the Biblical text with the freedom of a Protestant scholar, yet full credit must be given to a French Oratorian priest, Richard Simon (1638–1712), though not to the Church which instantly suppressed his work. Simon developed what was then an entirely new field of scholarship, the study of the actual texts and versions of the Bible. The author was expelled from the Oratory when he attempted to publish his conclusions, and his book was burnt. But it subsequently appeared under various disguises. The first was a beautifully printed Elzevir octavo, pleasantly entitled *Histoire de la Religion des Juifs, et de leur Etablissement en Espagne et autres parties de l'Europe où il se sont retirés aprés la Destruction de Jerusalem, écrite par Rabbi Moses Levi*. It also pretends to be printed in Amsterdam by Pierre de la Faille in 1680. Another work of his appeared in Rotterdam, and one would gather from the introduction that it was the work of a Protestant, for Richard Simon, having learned caution, appeared this time as Monsieur de Sainjore. On another occasion he assumed the title of Prieur de Bolleville. The real title of the original work is *L'Histoire critique du Vieux Testament*, and it is astonishingly accurate and objective for its time. Though Simon is said to have been of a quarrelsome disposition, nothing of that appears in his polished French and gentle suavity. Of particular interest is his treatment of the charge constantly made in Christian polemics that the Jews falsified the Scriptures to overcome their Christian adversaries. After examining all the facts, he delivers judgment in favour of the Jews against the Church Fathers, and actually claims that Christian polemics caused the Jews to correct corruptions in their text rather than create new ones.

In the eighteenth century an Italian scholar, Biagio Ugolini (*c.* 1700 to *c.* 1770) set out to collect together all the many works on Hebrew antiquities which had poured from the universities of Europe, Protestant as well as Roman Catholic, during the preceding two hundred years. The result was a work in thirty-four folio volumes entitled *Thesaurus Antiquitatum Sacrarum*, which contained the work of Buxtorf, Selden, Spencer, Wagenseil, and a hundred others. In addition, much was written by Ugolini himself including many translations of rabbinical texts. Nothing is known of his life—indeed, it is difficult to imagine he had any life outside the proof-room, so vast is his compendium—but it is commonly believed that he was a convert from Judaism.

While the range from Buxtorf to Surenhuis shows what was possible within the ranks of general Protestant orthodoxy all sorts of extravagancies were to be found among the wilder sects, especially in seventeenth-century England, where Biblical studies had a strong political flavour and the prophetic thought was easily father to the revolutionary wish. Yet it was these sects whose Biblical and millenarian dreams led to the first serious discussions of toleration and emancipation. As has happened elsewhere in Jewish affairs, events combined to produce results which none had directly intended. The battle against an established Church led to demands for religious toleration, and, in the end, the Jews benefited by this; Biblical literalism led to a search for the lost tribes, and an impatience to greet the return of the Messiah, but as the return of the Jews to England had to precede this event, the millenarians and such demanded that the doors be opened to them. Yet when they did openly return, it was in consequence of none of these interests or expectations, but as part of Cromwell's commercial policy, and without any formal act of admission.

Nevertheless, one feature was of permanent importance: the Jews came again to be associated in people's minds with their Biblical history. They came to be thought of as God's chosen people from whom His favour had been temporarily withdrawn, but who were still heirs to the promises made to their forefathers. This feeling underlies many of the pamphlets published at the time, and acted as a considerable political lever, even though it failed in the end to cause the kind of open and magnificent restoration of which Manasseh ben Israel and his Protestant supporters dreamed.

There was, however, another side to the consideration of the Jews as "the people of the Book." It left entirely on one side the development of post-Biblical Judaism. Though, while the Talmud was simply a book to abuse, it was no disadvantage that it should recede into the background, it is an important fact for the future, and for the history of emancipation, that early Protestantism did, in fact, mistake the nature of Judaism, even when it approved of it. It was only slowly that even the essential character of the actual Biblical legislation of the Pentateuch, as the religion of a community, came to be realised by a few; that the Talmud had developed this religion, both necessarily and logically, was realised by such free spirits as Bodin or Selden, neither of whom was either a minister of religion or a professor at a university under the control of a Church; but of those whose position tied them to a certain orthodoxy Surenhuis stands out in the liberality of his mind and the penetration of his understanding. In general it was the Judaism of the Bible which came back into favour; and this itself has considerable importance; for it meant the recognition that the Old Testament did not exist only as a quarry from which the Christians might dig proof-texts for their claims, but did also record the early history of the still-existing Jewish people. The series of works on *The Republic of Moses* mark a new epoch in Christian Biblical understanding. What was still lacking was the realisation of the principle of growth and interpretation as an essential part of the Sinaitic revelation; for scholars were still using the works of the rabbis mainly as additional explanations of the meaning of Biblical texts.

Among the many expositions of the Republic of Moses, there is one which stands out. It is the *Nova Solyma*, and its interest is that, in the manner of More's *Utopia*, it attempts to describe in novel form what the Republic would be like, by imagining it as still existing. Actually, its author exhibits more familiarity with the Republic of Plato than with that of Moses. The work is by Samuel Gott (1613–71), a Cambridge friend of Milton, and it was unfortunately published just as the Civil War reached its climax in 1648, so that it attracted no attention. It was only rediscovered some forty years ago. *Nova Solyma* is the capital of a Jewish State, and is visited by two young Englishmen fifty years after its re-establishment. The Jews have accepted their Messiah and been restored to their country, which is a magnificent example of civilisation, stability and prosperity. Incidentally, no particular emphasis is laid on this acceptance of Christianity; it is the subject merely of passing reference. But the new Jewish community, which is charmingly and romantically described, owes more to Plato than to Moses. The names of the characters are nearly all classical, the landscape is classical, and, though the government is republican and a model of justice and temperance, there is little to show that it owes anything either to Moses or the rabbis. Cicero and Epicurus would have been more at home in its dignified palaces than Jochanan ben Zakkai or Maimonides. And even Moses might have been a little puzzled at times!

The idealism and unreality of much of the Protestant philo-Jewish feeling was a political misfortune. For it left the political and most of the religious field for another century and a half to the more realistic but unfriendly appraisers of the actual state of contemporary Jewry, who were aware of the effects on Jewish life of centuries of persecution and restriction, but felt no sympathy with it or responsibility for it. It will be enough to take a couple of examples of this feature in writers of widely separated dates. The Reverend John Weemse of Lathocker in Scotland, Prebend of Durham, published in 1636 a treatise on *The Four Degenerate Sons* (the Atheist, the Magician, the Idolator and the Jew) in which he discusses "whether the Jews are to be suffered in a Christian common wealth or not."[8] He begins well by saying that "the Jews are to be tollerated among Christians, when they are out of the Covenant" (for which he adopts the word from Hosea, *lognammi*) "as they did tolerate us Gentiles when we were out of the Covenant." The parallel he follows fairly closely. Jews who rail against Christ and the Christians are "the Synagogue of Satan," and should be put to death by the Christian magistrate. Those who are Jews by birth and religion, "but not in affection" (probably equal to the modern word "affectation" and a reference to Christian dissenting sects who claimed to be the true Israel), "if they dwell peaceably

amongst us, and abstaine from offence" are to be accepted.
But he proposes for them a Christian version of the Noachian
Commandments: "some short principles of Christian religion should be taught them, as the Gentiles who were
advenae portae learned the seven precepts of Noah." He
admits that these Jews are to be accepted because there is
hope of their full conversion. They are, however, to be
received on conditions. There shall be no compulsory conversions; and they may practise their Jewish customs, and have
synagogues, in order to read the Law, "for the word of God
is still the word of God, although they abuse it to a wrong
end." But they must do nothing offensive to Christianity.
A hundred years later, J. Jodocus Beck, in *Tractatus de
Juribus Judaeorum* (1731), likewise discusses whether a
Christian State may admit Jews, and decides that it can
do so only on full medieval conditions, with special dress and
so on, and with all cases involving Christians as well as Jews
judged by Roman Law.[9] Yet it was to be expected that in
the general atmosphere of interest in Judaism and things
Jewish which pervades the seventeenth and eighteenth
centuries, some individuals should, at some time and in
spite of historic Christian prejudice, draw from the new
interest in Hebrew and rabbinical studies a basic revision
of the conventional attitude towards Jewish destiny and
religion. It is, perhaps, not surprising that the men to do so
should so often be themselves outside the bounds of conventional religion. One such was an Irishman, John Toland
(1670–1722), an English Deist, and a vigorous and volumin-
ous pamphleteer on an immense variety of political, religious
and other subjects.

In a book entitled *Nazarenus*, and published in 1718,
Toland makes the first serious study of Judaic Christianity.
He identifies it with Ebionism, and claims that the right in-
terpretation of the apostolic age is that Judaic and Gentile
Christianity were planned as two societies living side by side,
the former still observing the Law, the latter the Noachic
Commandments. For, following certain medieval Jewish
critics, he identified the laws of the Council of Jerusalem in

Acts xv with those commandments given to all the sons of men. He holds that the Judeo-Christians were never intended to abandon the Law, and that their having been made to do so was a great calamity. Toland seems also to have had some understanding of the basic fact that Judaism is essentially the religion of a community, for he writes:[10] "I maintain the Plan given by Moses never to have been wholly, nor indeed in any degree of perfection, establish'd in Judaea; and that if it once had, it cou'd never have been afterwards destroy'd, either by the internal sedition of subjects, or the external violence of enemies, but shou'd have lasted as long as mankind." And at the end he says:

"Now if you'll suppose with me this pre-eminence and immortality of the MOSAIC REPUBLIC in its original purity, it will follow that . . . if [the Jews] ever happen to be resettl'd in Palestine upon their original foundation, which is not at all impossible; they will then, by reason of their excellent constitution be much more populous, rich and powerful than any other nation now in the world. I wou'd have you consider, whether it be not both the interest and duty of Christians to assist them in regaining their country."

He promised a book on the Mosaic Republic, but unfortunately it was never written or, at least, never published. Still, Toland's views remained more than a century in advance of his time.

It was not only the theologians and religious writers, however, who showed an interest in things Jewish. The spread of printing and the multiplication of books greatly increased the demand among the cultured classes for works of objective information, especially such as dealt with anything which was curious or novel. This demand produced a number of books of considerable value, dealing with the lives of contemporary Jews; and though they were generally written from a professedly Christian standpoint, they were not primarily concerned to do more than divert their readers.

In 1675 Lancelot Addison went out to the Barbary Coast
(i.e. Tangiers) as a naval chaplain, and there made a study
of the Jews of North Africa, which he published under the
title of *The Present State of the Jews of Barbary*. The accuracy
of the work is perhaps unfairly judged by that which renders
it still interesting—a superb frontispiece representing a
Barbary Jew, carrying a spear, and wearing only a vast
headdress of ostrich feathers and a meagre loin-covering
of the same!

Of much fuller interest is *Jüdische Merckwuerdigkeiten*, by
Johann Jacob Schudt of Frankfurt, published in 1714, and
concerned with what is *"curieus und denckwürdig"* in the
customs of contemporary Jews all over the world. He even
discusses whether the lost ten tribes are to be found in
America, and decides against it![11] Another work of the same
kind is the *Kirchliche Verfassung der heutigen Juden sonderlich
derer in Deutschland*, by J. C. G. Bodenschatz, published in
1748, and enriched with thirty copper plates of Jewish
customs. These, together with Bernard Picart's more famous
plates of Jewish life in Holland (1725), form some of our
earliest non-satirical illustrations of Jewish life.

These works were partly made possible by the serious
studies in Jewish history which were beginning to appear,
and which also strove to preserve the objectivity of that
excellent period of scholarship. The greatest of these is
*L'Histoire et la Religion des Juifs depuis Jésus Christ jusqu'à
present*, by Jacques Basnage de Beauval (1653–1723), a
Dutch pastor, diplomat and prolific writer. There is an interesting contrast between Basnage's own attitude to the
sufferings of the Jews and that of the Reverend Thomas
Taylor, his pompous English translator. The latter still
speaks the conventional language of the Church in his dedi-
cation of his work to the Bishop of Winchester. He considers
it an argument for the truth of Christianity to "lay before
the scoffers and despisers of our religion" this story of the
Jews "wandring and dispersed into all corners of the
earth by the Malediction of Heaven . . . a standing evidence
of Divine Vengeance on Unbelief and an Indelible

Monument of the Truth of Christianity."[12] But Basnage himself writes in a different tone:

> "I content myself with pointing out known facts; I am so far from intending to render the [Jewish] people contemptible by a description of their miserable condition, that I consider that one should regard it as one of those prodigies which one admires without wholly understanding. . . . The attention and the pity of Christians should be aroused for men whom God has preserved for so long in spite of a burden of suffering under which any people other than they would have been completely entombed."[13]

Like the work of Richard Simon, this book also has a curious history. Its objectivity did not please the Jesuits, and they forged an edition of it, in which views which might be thought offensive to the Roman Church were altered or omitted. That they should have taken such trouble shows the popularity of the subject. The work is of considerable size, and was first published in 1706. It appeared in English in a folio of seven hundred and fifty closely printed pages in 1708. The Jesuit edition appeared in 1710. Mr. Basnage's reply, "reclaimed and re-established by its real author, Mr. Basnage, against the anonymous and falsified edition," appeared in 1711, and was followed by a new and enlarged edition of the whole work in 1716.

National histories followed rapidly, in England, Switzerland and elsewhere, for the eighteenth century had a passion for history. In the middle of the century appeared in innumerable volumes the first attempt at a universal history; and the two volumes consecrated to the Jews have this interest (apart from their evident sympathy with Jewish suffering and their feeling that Providence is on its mettle to compensate them with a glorious future) that they were written, after his exposure and repentance, by that amazing imposter, George Psalmanazar (1679–1763). Psalmanazar, whose real name and origin are unknown, invented a complete alphabet, language, grammar and religion of his own, with costume and diet thrown in, which for many years he persuaded the savants of Europe to accept as the language and religion of Formosa. After his exposure he became an accomplished Hebraist, and wrote, among other things, the history of the Jews. He died in an odour of sanctity and the arms of Dr. Johnson!

On the background of the work done by the orientalists, the theologians, the political theorists, the historians and the authors of travel books, the final steps towards emancipation were taken under the influence of Rousseau rather than of religion. Jews became beneficiaries of a general atmosphere of toleration, when they had failed to obtain assistance from a religious affection directed especially at themselves. It was fortunate for Jewry that just at this time there should appear in Berlin a young German Jew, Moses Mendelssohn, who, by the beauty of his personal character, the eminence of his intellectual gifts, and the wide range of his philosophic and religious understanding, stood as the living symbol of what an emancipated Jew might be to all those circles which were susceptible to enlightened ideas.

A new study of the Jewish question, free from the prejudices imported by the long Christian tradition, at last enabled some in the eighteenth century to realise that the faults of the Jews were the product of their history, not of the viciousness of their religion. This has never found nobler expression than in the closing paragraphs of the appeal of Abbé Grégoire for the emancipation of the Jews of France in 1789:[14]

"O Nations, for eighteen centuries you have trampled under foot the relics of Israel. The divine vengeance has visited them with severity; but have *you* been appointed to carry out the sentence? . . . Judge this Nation no more save by its future; but if you must turn your eyes once more on the past crimes of the Jews and their present corruption, then let it be to deplore the work of *your* hands. Responsible for their vices, be now responsible for their virtues . . . pay the debt of yourselves and your ancestors. Children of the same Father, tear out of your hearts every pretext for hating your brothers who will be united with you one day in the same fold. Open to them a refuge where they can rest their heads and dry their tears. And may the day come when the Jew, moved in his turn with tender love for the Christian, may embrace in me his fellow citizen and his friend."

The background of the Abbé Grégoire's appeal was to be found in Berlin and in the circles of Moses Mendelssohn; and if the closing words of the Abbé reflected admirably *les panaches* beloved of the French, the opening words of *Ueber die bürgerliche Verbesserung der Juden* of the friend of Mendelssohn, Christian Wilhelm Dohm (1751–1820), equally well reflected the thoroughness of the German:

"The Governments of all the great European powers seem now to be basically agreed that a steady increase of population is the necessary foundation of the greatest common good. We believe that when we can secure a steady increase of numbers we shall best secure the stability of our civic community, and protect it against external attack, develop our natural resources and increase the manufactures which grow from them, extend our international trade, and in general secure the most certain advantage to our industry and the common welfare of our citizens."

The appeal of Dohm was, on the surface at any rate, an appeal entirely to self-interest. The more citizens, the more prosperity. Why then do you not make the Jews among you into citizens? He proposed to give them all rights, except that political enfranchisement would be delayed until they had some political experience. Unfortunately, Dohm referred to Jews as "*asiatische Flüchtlinge,*" and so lent colour to the nineteenth-century denial that the Jewish people were, like ourselves, an integral part of Mediterranean-European culture. The appeal of Dohm was followed by many others, written by both Jews and Christians; and his work soon became known outside Germany. In fact, as has been said, it was in French emancipation that it first had its full effect.

Emancipation, as it gradually came in western Europe, was affected not only by the humanitarian appeal of Grégoire or the utilitarian appeal of Dohm; it was equally affected by developments in western European Jewry, especially in Berlin. When in the French Constituent Assembly Clermont-Tonnerre cried that it was necessary *"tout accorder aux Juifs comme individus, et tout leur refuser comme nation,"* he was determining prophetically the lines of a division which was to rend Jewish life for more than a century; and which in fact is still unsolved to-day. That there were Jews who were prepared to accept this emancipation *comme individus* was partly due to the inertia and decadence which had overcome orthodoxy, exhausted by the long centuries of its humiliation and persecution; but was due still more to the new interpretations of Judaism enthusiastically and optimistically proclaimed by the circle which drew its inspiration from Moses Mendelssohn and a group of his followers who were known as the *Meassefim,* the Collectors.

The "disputation" between Mendelssohn and Lavater, which took the form of an exchange of letters between 1769 and 1771, was the introduction to a new epoch in Jewish apologetic.[15] Gone were the serried confrontations of Biblical texts. Mendelssohn approached the task with regret and refused it as an equal, in terms so courteous that they drew from Lavater a sincere and honourable apology. Mendelssohn showed himself at once an enlightened philosopher and a convinced advocate of a religion which he claimed to be at once national and rational. For he himself managed to combine in his thought a belief in the historical fact of the Sinaitic revelation and its permanent validity for Israel with a rational acceptance of the thesis that an exclusive religion cannot be true, and that in the thought of true Judaism all the inhabitants of the earth are destined to eternal bliss. But the position was too complicated for his followers easily to maintain.

In consequence, it was the individualistic side of Judaism

which was most frequently advanced, and found immortal expression in Lessing's *Nathan der Weise*. This led to a second new line of apologetic in the systematic presentation of Talmudic teaching on the ethics of the individual. A good example is the reply of J. Wolf and G. Salomon to Professor Rühs and Fries: *Der Charakter des Judenthums*, 1817. But this reduction of the Talmud to a textbook of personal ethics, valuable as it was as a reply to a Buxtorf, a Bodenschatz or an Eisenmenger, lent an unfortunate support to the individualism of emancipation, and to the idea that Judaism was "only another religion, just like Christianity."

While these attitudes undoubtedly won for the Jews the support of the small enlightened and intellectual circle in which they were produced, they found little response in the general political and ecclesiastical world. Consequently, they served to disarm the Jews rather more than they armed their friends; and the presentation of Judaism as an ethical-rational system, whose rationalism could be accepted by any philosopher and whose ethics were identical with those of Christianity, widened the breach between the small middle-class western European groups of emancipated Jews and the immense masses of Jewry, East and West. But while the breach was widened within Jewry, the gulf was narrowed between these emancipated Jews and the dominant religion, whether Roman Catholic or Protestant. For, since both the latter maintained unchanged their missionary activities, and since the political world would not believe in the ethical identity of Judaism and Christianity unless the Jews proved that identity by willingly accepting baptism, there was a steady stream of converts from these "enlightened" Jewish circles into the Churches.

This tendency Jewish orthodoxy was unable to impede. For it had become too completely out of touch with that Western world in which the Western Jew was coming to be at home, even to be able to explain itself to Western Jews, let alone to Western Christians. Western Jewry in its turn became so remote from the Talmudic discussions in which Eastern Jewry still delighted that when in the end of the nineteenth century Rohling launched his attacks on the Talmud, and proclaimed that it taught ritual murder and encouraged every kind of malpractice towards Christians, Viennese Jews were overcome with shame and horror, knowing nothing of its contents themselves and not believing that a Canon of the Church and a Professor of the Imperial and Royal University of Prague would deliberately lie. It required the courage and knowledge of a young Viennese rabbi of Polish (Galician) origin, Dr. Joseph Bloch, to force Rohling to eat his words. But it is unfair to blame Jewry for this situation. The circumstances which confronted it in the eighteenth–nineteenth centuries had this basic difference from the situation which confronted Christendom in the battle for reformation which attended the breakdown of the Middle Ages. Christians were not then living as minorities in the midst of a non-Christian environment whose political and religious leaders watched with unfriendly eyes every move, seized with joy on every confession of weakness, unscrupulously exploited every failure and, at the same time, dangled before the eyes of Jewish youth the attractions of entry by baptism into a world which seemed—and sometimes was—far richer than that offered them by the ghettoes of their fathers or the sorrows of the Russian Pale. But this was the situation in which the battle for the reform of Jewry took place. The prejudiced misrepresentations in missionary literature—whether Protestant or Roman Catholic—paralleled the political development of a new antisemitism. It is surprising only that so many Jews stood firm and embarked on the difficult task of trying to modernise orthodoxy itself.

Their task was made more difficult by the fact that Biblical scholarship, in spite of its immense advances in the sphere of knowledge, showed, on the whole, little interest in the spirit behind the texts it so sedulously examined. The bare bones of Jewish belief and practice in Old Testament and Talmudic times were, on the whole, objectively disentangled and described by both Jewish and Christian scholars. But the former had sometimes as little sympathetic insight into the spirit behind them as the latter, and both were content to leave orthodox practices untouched in the church or synagogue while they dissected them in the university and the scientific periodical. The general environment was secularist; it was an age of reason rather than belief, which yet accepted adherence to a religious institution and attendance at its services as a sign of social respectability.

Jewish history as well as the Jewish religion were examined with the same scrupulously honest but, on the whole, unimaginative approach, and interpreted in the light of the rationalist and "scientific" spirit of the age. It might well have appeared certain to the emancipated Jews of 1850 that the long and tragic history of Jewry was at last completed, and that contemporary progress, toleration and reason would soon undo the work of centuries of ignorance, superstition and fanaticism. And yet the reaction was already seething beneath the surface. If on the Christian side a new wave of antisemitism was being prepared, on the Jewish side the elements which were to ensure the survival of Jewry and of Judaism were already beginning to stir.

It would have seemed fantastic to the great Jewish historian Heinrich Graetz (1817–91) that eastern European Jewry could undo the work which the individualism of Western emancipation had done—still more fantastic that it should desire to do so. That it should be right in so doing would have seemed to him incredible.

Whereas in the pre-emancipation period it was the change in the Christian attitude which we were following, this time we need to look at the situation from a Jewish as well as a Christian standpoint. It is difficult to select from the material available the key-points which mark an epoch. But the most substantial of the early Jewish formulations of the new attitude was, perhaps, *Rome and Jerusalem*, by Moses Hess (1812–75). Hess was a German Jew, a socialist who had at one time been a collaborator of Marx and Engels. Exiled from Germany for his share in the abortive revolution of 1848, he settled in France, a country for which he always retained the liveliest affection and which he expected to be the prime

FJC

mover in Jewish restoration. Hess gives this analysis of the force of Eastern and Western Jewry:[16]

"The rigid crust of orthodox Jewry will melt when the spark of Jewish patriotism, now smouldering under it, is kindled into a sacred fire which will herald the coming of the Spring and the resurrection of our nation to a new life. On the other hand, Occidental Judaism is surrounded by an almost indissolvable crust, composed of the dead residue of the first manifestation of the modern spirit, from the inorganic chalk deposit of an extinct rationalistic enlightenment. This crust will not be melted by the fire of Jewish patriotism; it can only be broken by an external pressure under the weight of which everything which has no future must give up its existence. In contradistinction to orthodoxy, which cannot be destroyed by an external force without at the same time endangering the embryo of Jewish Nationalism that slumbers within it, the hard covering that surrounds the hearts of our cultured Jews will be shattered only by a blow from without, one that world events are already preparing; and which will probably fall in the near future."

The revival of Judaism and the revival of a Jewish nation went hand in hand in his mind; but it soon emerged that many of the battles of early Zionists were with the orthodox Synagogue; and the supporters of Zionism among the rabbis, though by no means negligible, were a minority. Two more works can be quoted as showing the flowering of the seed sown by Hess. Both are short, and both were originally written in Russia, though one was in the German language—*Auto-emancipation*, by Leo Pinsker, written in 1882, and *Jewish History; an Essay in the Philosophy of History* by Simon Dubnow, written some fifteen years later. In these two works the continuity and the national character of the centuries of Jewish life stood forth clearly. Both were written by "enlightened" Jews who were by-products of the Russian Haskalah. But in neither case were they written by "citizens" of their country. And in consequence they had escaped the weakness of the western European reform movements, based on the individualism of emancipation in western European society.

In the first part of *Auto-emancipation*, Pinsker has these searching words:

"That which hinders the Jews most from any desire for a proper national existence, is that they feel no need for it. And, not content with feeling no such need, they even dispute the legitimacy of the idea itself."

It was here that Pinsker saw the spiritual malady within Russian Jewry; it was to create in them a legitimate pride in the glory of their history that Dubnow wrote his superb essay.

The rediscovery that the Jews were a people was proceeding simultaneously in various Christian circles in various countries. The uncertainty as to the future of Syria after Mehmet Ali had been dispossessed of the country by the European Powers in 1840 led to various projects for the restoration of Palestine to the Jews. Laurence Oliphant in England, Ernest Laharanne in France, Dr. A. F. Petavel in Switzerland were only some among the many who paralleled the work of Hess and his successors from the Christian side.

The Christian rediscovery of Judaism proceeded more slowly. Immensely important scientific work was done, and innumerable details of rabbinic law and practice were explained and put into their right perspective. But the spark was not kindled.

Finally, in some measure the debt owed by Christianity to Judaism was repaid by the fact that that interpretation which Jewish orthodoxy could not give for itself, was first given to it by an English Unitarian, Dr. Travers Herford. Many had brought knowledge to bear upon the subject. Dr. Herford brought understanding. After the learned works of Schurer and Weber, of Oesterley and Robinson, Pharisaic Judaism was suddenly made to live by the appearance in 1912 of *Pharisaism*. Since then other works have come from his pen, and other authors, especially the American Christian George Foote Moore, have added to his work. It may be that at times they are too enthusiastic; at times perhaps they over-emphasised the virtues of the system they described, but for the first time the Christian world was made to see a living, creative and fascinating spiritual religion in the Pharisaism which the Christian Gospels had so one-sidedly and completely condemned, and which in consequence had remained completely unknown to the Christian world—and indeed to a good deal of the Jewish world.

Three years before the work of Travers Herford on rabbinic Judaism appeared that of Claude Montefiore on the Christian Gospels. Both authors have been violently attacked by their own side for being unduly favourable to the other. There may be some truth in the attacks, as well as much exaggeration. But the two together marked a new epoch, and however much what they have written may be challenged by subsequent ages, what they have done is of permanent importance. For the first time the rôles in the age-long controversy between Jews and Christians have been reversed. The Gentile has set out to show his Christian contemporaries the spiritual values of Judaism; the Jew has set out to show his Jewish contemporaries the spiritual insights of Christianity.

What still remains to be done is the creation of unity between the religious and the national understanding of Jewish history, and the acceptance within the non-Jewish world of the combination of non-cosmopolitan universalism, and non-exclusive particularism, which is at once the peculiar character of Judaism and the basis of the contribution of the Jews as a people to the rich variety of the world's civilisations.

Part Four

PRESENT TASKS

CHAPTER SIX

PROBLEMS OF A NEW CHRISTIAN ATTITUDE TO JUDAISM

ONE OF THE MOST unhappy aspects of the present situation, as it affects those Churches whose scholars have been free from doctrinal and ecclesiastical prohibitions in their search into the origins of Christianity and their examination of the documents in which those origins are recorded, is that the results of their researches have to so small a degree been transmitted into the body of teaching and institutional expressions of the Churches of which they are members. Those Churches which maintain intact their doctrine of the verbal infallibility of the Scriptures are not affected by the problem. They have other problems to face, but with these I am not concerned. But for me as an Anglican, the situation is become spiritually intolerable. In theological colleges and universities, in books and scientific periodicals, an entirely new conception of the nature of the writings of the Old and New Testaments has become a universally accepted basis for further research. But there is no trace of this conception either in the doctrines of the Anglican Church or in the use of the Scriptures in worship, and there is very little in religious education.

It is certainly not a question of the Church trimming her sails to every new school of interpretation, and constantly changing her beliefs or amending her Scriptures at the whim of those interpreters who are at any moment fashionable. The results of any such method of adjustment would be both ludicrous and chaotic. But while the latest

conclusions of scholars have only a transitory validity, the
conception that these conclusions do, in fact, have only a
transitory validity, that they ought to have only a transitory
validity, and that it is the will of God that they shall have
only a transitory validity, because the duty of interpretation
according to the best knowledge available at the time is a
continuous duty; this is a new doctrine of the meaning of
the Scriptures as spiritual, as profound, and as rich as the
old doctrine of verbal inspiration. If it were universally
taught in the Churches that in the Scriptures we had
interpretations of revelation, not revelation itself, the way
would be open for the fundamental changes which are
necessary, and the way would also be open to making
interpretation a living reality as well as a continuous and
corporate responsibility of the Churches. I realise, of course,
that such an alteration of the doctrine of the Scriptures
would affect other doctrines also. It could not be combined
with the maintenance of the equally important doctrine
that the last word was said about the nature of God and the
relationship of the Holy Trinity at the Council of Nicæa. I
am, in fact, arguing that the Churches should in modern
form teach what Pharisaism taught about the traditions
of the Elders—that is, that the discoveries of men about
the nature of the Universe and its Creator form a continuous
process, which is never arrested save by human blindness,
fear and arrogance; and that all that men have so far
expressed on these, the deepest subjects of life, are interpretations which are valid for their age and generation,
and signposts to new discoveries and new understanding
for future generations, signposts along a road which never
ends through a universe which is ever unfolding. But at the
moment I am concerned with only one small field in which
the need for such reinterpretation is focused on one particular issue—the relations of Calvary to Sinai, of the Church
to the Synagogue.

If the thesis which has been unfolded in the preceding
chapters of this book is, in its major lines, correct, then
the problem which is posed to any sincere Christian is both

inescapable and agonising. In our own day and within our own civilisation, more than six million deliberate murders are the consequence of teaching about Jews for which the Christian Church is ultimately responsible, and of an attitude to Judaism which is not only maintained by all the Christian Churches, but has its ultimate resting place in the teaching of the New Testament itself. Of course, so long as the Churches are in a position to maintain that that teaching is right, and that the contents of the New Testament on the subject of Judaism are unquestionably the whole truth, there is nothing to be said or done. The consequences are regrettable, but also inevitable, and the ultimate fault lies not with the Churches, but with the Jews. But what of those Christians who cannot sincerely maintain such a position? Can they any longer escape their responsibility for doing something about a tradition, however ancient or revered, which has produced such results?

Of what value is the freedom given to scholarship to search and to declare what it believes to be true, if scholars assume no moral responsibility for the results of their researches? And here the charge, which lies indeed on all the Christian congregations involved, must be held to lie with especial responsibility on the shoulders of Christian scholarship. It has so far refused the responsibility, but history will not thereby hold it innocent.

There are three spheres in which a profound change is needed; in the sphere of the official attitude of the Church to the Synagogue; in the use of the Scriptures in the services of the Church; and in religious education.

The attitude of the Church still rests on the assumption that the Church has inherited, and expresses in its life and teaching, everything which was valid in the Old Testament and the Synagogue; and that Judaism has retained only the husks and external forms of the Sinaitic revelation. In saying that in Calvary Sinai is "fulfilled," the Church understands that Sinai is "replaced," and has no further independent validity. All that it had is included in Calvary. It is a natural consequence of this belief that churchmen should see their whole duty to Jewry as confined to the duty of converting Jews to that type of Christianity they themselves profess, and that they should believe that any such conversion is conversion from what was wholly error to what is wholly truth. To this end, the Churches have either maintained themselves, or have extended official patronage to, missions whose task is this conversion. I am not concerned here with the right of any Jew who is sincerely convinced of the truth of Christianity to change his religion; I am not even concerned with the right of any individual Christian to seek to bring his Jewish friends to the same way of thinking as himself. Those are rights inherent in the very essence of religious freedom, and belong equally to Jews, Christians, and members of all other faiths or philosophies. But we are dealing with a different matter in dealing with the official attitude of the Churches.

To-day the mission to the Jews is the Cinderella among the missions, at any rate of the Protestant Churches. But this is more due to its evidently limited success than to any radical change in opinion as to its necessity. It is, of course, true that during the centuries many Jews have become sincere and devout Christians and, in view of frequent Jewish assertions, it is well to remind ourselves that this is so. But it is equally true that many such converts have not been the result of direct missionary activity, and that the result of the Christian missions themselves should give Christians cause for a profound re-examination of their rightness as the form of approach of the one religion to the other.

We forget that the mission to the Jews is the most sustained and all-embracing of all the missions of the Christian Church. It starts from the moment of the separation of the two religions, and has continued now for nearly two thousand years. During the greater part of this period the majority of the Jewish people have actually been living as minorities in Christian parishes, in direct and continuous contact with Christian laity and clergy, many of whom were living saintly lives. Until the twentieth century, any Jew could benefit himself materially as well as (as the Christian Church believed) spiritually by passage to Christianity. Only a tiny minority have done so.

When we examine the record of the missions to the Jews, there are two facts which appear to me even more significant than their extremely limited success. The first is that I do not believe there is any other activity of the Church in which good men from deeply religious motives have done such wicked things. In spite of all modern attempts at whitewash, the Spanish Inquisition remains an appalling monument of the evil good men will do, and the greater part of its activities were due to the determination with which Jews, baptised by force—whether social or physical—retained their affection for Judaism. But the Spanish Inquisition is not alone; all through the early and middle ages of the Church, forced baptisms took place under conditions of revolting cruelty— again mental or physical. The literature of the Church directed at Judaism has already been discussed; but we must remember also the continuous abuse and misrepresentation from the pulpit.

Nor can we shelter ourselves by the comforting belief that all these things happened a long time ago. In our own day we can witness the complacent attitude of certain missions to the enticement of children away from their parents which has earned no general condemnation from the Churches. At the beginning of the century it was a common practice to bribe with clothing, sweets and toys the children of penniless immigrants from eastern Europe in the slums of London. There it broke into an open scandal, and the facts are known, and the more honest of the missionary societies involved finally acknowledged them.[1] To what extent the same thing may have happened elsewhere I do not know. Just before 1939 certain missionaries in central Europe, with the approval of their missions, persuaded desperate mothers that they would take their children out of reach of Hitler if the mother would sign a document (sometimes at any rate in English so that the mother did not understand it). The document gave the missionary the right to bring the child up in the Christian faith. In some cases the child was the son of orthodox parents and had celebrated his *Bar Mitzvah*, so that there is no question but that the mother did not know what she was signing. Finally, there are the cases of children who were sheltered in Christian homes during the Nazi occupation, and who are refused restoration to the Jewish community. In any individual case the issues may be difficult to decide, but the overall picture is one which should make Christians reflect seriously on the background causes of—to say the least—so dubiously moral a situation.

The second fact is equally striking. In the long and tragic course of the history of the Jews among the Christian nations, there are three accusations which have been levelled against them which have caused more bloodshed than any others. All three are false; *but all three were "proved" by the evidence of Jewish converts to Christianity.* I know that to some sincere and distinguished Christians this fact appears totally irrelevant; they are content to balance it against the number of sincere converts who have led admirably Christian lives. But I cannot feel that the matter can be disposed of so easily. Believing as I do that Christianity is true, I see no difficulty in believing that is has attracted Jews sincerely, and that they have found joy, peace and power in its adoption. What I cannot see is how, if the theology which underlies the missionary attitude is the right one officially to adopt, it could have produced these contrary effects. They deny the rationality of the universe. To believe that the fulfilment of the will of God could lead to such results is to believe in the totally irrational; whereas to believe that men, seeking to fulfil the will of God, and actually doing the opposite, should produce terrible results would appear a logical consequence of believing that fulfilling or not fulfilling the will of God is not a trifle but a matter of the highest importance.

Nor can the matter be dismissed by saying that there are frauds in every section of humanity. In the cases under consideration the vital point is that these converts were officially accepted by the Church as sincere, and officially protected and supported.

The three charges in question are *the blood accusation*—the charge that Jews murdered Christian children in order to get blood for ritual purposes; the charge that Jews were organised with the lepers in *a conspiracy to poison the wells* of Europe; and the charge that the Jews were organised in *a secret international organisation plotting the overthrow of Christendom* and the domination of the world.

The first accusation of ritual murder is connected with the finding of the body of a Christian boy, William, at Norwich in 1144. It happens to be a case of which we have a long and contemporary account.[2] The whole introduction of a ritual and communal element into the affair was due to the evidence of a Jewish convert, Theobald, a monk of Cambridge, who told a long and apparently substantial story of the annual securing of blood in order to make unleavened bread for Passover. In the nineteenth-century revival of antisemitism in Austria, two Jewish converts played a similar rôle, August Brimann and Paulus Meyer; and the latter produced a story that he himself, when a young mhassidic student, had actually taken part in a ritual Curder in Russia. Both men were again and again supported, and their characters and actions endorsed, by responsible members of the Roman Catholic Church. Both were ultimately proved to be complete liars and charlatans.[3]

The suspicion that Jews had poisoned the wells when any plague broke out in the insanitary slums of a medieval city appears first in the eleventh century. But it was at the beginning of the fourteenth that "proof" of this was produced by two Jewish converts "translating" a Hebrew letter which had been discovered in the coffers of a Jew, Bananias, in Anjou.[4] When thirty years later the Black Death slew a third of the population of Europe, the case was held to be proved against the Jews, and thousands of them paid with their lives for the treachery of the apostate.

The charge that Jews were engaged in a secret world plot also can be traced to the medieval period; but it became a serious matter only in nineteenth-century Russia, when a Jewish convert to Orthodoxy, Hugo Brafmann, produced *The Book of the Kahal*, which was supposed to contain the minutes of the secret meetings of the Jewish elders of the different communities in the Russian Pale. The book was officially accepted as authentic, and widely circulated at Government expense to departments and police head-quarters. It proved the political, though not the literary, background for the acceptance of the authenticity of the *Protocols of the Elders of Zion*, themselves in all probability the work of a Russian Jew converted to Roman Catholicism, Dr. de Cyon, written as a satire on the world intrigues and ambitions—as de Cyon saw them—of the Russian Minister of Finance, Count Witte. [5]

A collection of evidence from all centuries of the activities of converts against the members of the faith which they had left would make terrible reading; for I have but given the few whose work produced such outstanding consequences as the deaths of thousands—even tens of thousands—of their fellows. It appears to me incredible that such consequences could have resulted if the Christian attitude to Judaism which led to them did, in fact, conform to the will of God.

One final point is the rarity with which evidence in the contrary sense is to be found—of Christian converts from Judaism coming forward to testify to the falsity of these charges, or even, in a more general sense, to attack or even deplore the Christian attitude to their late brethren, the ghetto, the badge, the absence of civil rights, the expulsions and humiliations which Jews suffered in all the countries of Christendom. I know of no medieval case in which converts came forward voluntarily to intercede for their brethren, though there is one case where they denied the charge of ritual murder when summoned by the Emperor to do so. Among the mass of seventeenth- and eighteenth-century literature of the type discussed in the previous chapter, there is a small volume, *Kurzer Entwurf der Erklärung Jüdischer Gebräuche*, of Karl Anton, which is distinguished by the fact that it is written by a convert from Judaism, and yet defends the Jewish people against the charges made against them.[6] In the nineteenth century a group of fifty-eight converts signed a manifesto against the ritual murder accusation in Damascus in 1840; Dr. J. A. W. Neander, Professor of Church History at the University of Berlin, likewise protested, and another convert, Dr. Chwolson of the University of St. Petersburg, not only published a valuable study exposing the falseness of the accusation, but throughout his life was ready to rise in the defence of his Jewish brethren. But these are pitifully few to set in the opposite scale. It remains true that the greatest traitors to the Jewish people throughout their history have been Jews who have professed the Christian religion, and have been supported by the Christian Churches in the libels they have issued. There were distinguished orientalists in the academic life of nineteenth-century Germany who were converts, and it may not have been always true that they accepted baptism because it was the only door through which they could enter academic life; in the mission fields there have been men of undoubted saintliness, whose acceptance of Christianity had brought them intense personal suffering instead of academic honours, and whose sincerity has been beyond question. Why not? There is nothing strange in this to one who believes Christianity to be true. But it cannot answer the question asked above: how, if the theological attitude of the Church to the Synagogue be that which conforms to the purpose of God, can the other side be true—the deep stain of blood, the wall of intolerable lies, which stands between the peoples of the two faiths through the action of men who professed themselves Christians?

I have had some contact with the other missionary fields of the Christian Church, and I do not believe that any parallel to this general story of the mission to the Jews could be found elsewhere. There have, of course, been changes in the missionary approach; the attitude to other religions has changed from a general condemnation to an attempt at understanding; medical and educational work has come to be done more objectively and with less deliberate conversional intention. But all through their career the missions in Asia, Africa and elsewhere have produced men who have been outstanding servants of their still unconverted brethren, and outspoken champions and interpreters of their people to the Western world. One has only to think of such men as Dr. Aggrey of Africa, Dr. Datta of India, and Dr. T. Z. Koo of China. I know of some but very few such products of the missions to the Jews.

Half a century ago it would have appeared desirable for the members of any Church to convert other Christians to their own denomination; and official missions were maintained to this end. To-day only the Roman Catholic Church maintains this attitude; the other Churches have substituted the ecumenical movement for these activities. To suggest that the ecumenical idea should be extended also to the Synagogue is not easy. The common basis of the Churches united in the ecumenical movement is faith in Jesus Christ in the full Nicene sense. Even the Unitarian is considered to be outside the full Christian fold. How much more the Synagogue in which Jesus of Nazareth has no official place at all? And yet, if there is anything in the thesis of the first chapter, the only right attitude is one which recognises the equality of the Synagogue as the vehicle of a divine purpose still in process of fulfilment, the recipient of a still valid divine revelation.

We are, however, still a long way from the time when discussions of actual organisational relations are practical politics. The attitude out of which they would naturally emerge still needs to be created; and that involves a profound change in thinking. Moreover, this change is needed on both sides. It would be an illusion to believe that the Synagogue of to-day would find the recognition of the truth of the Church any easier to accept than would the Church the truth of the Synagogue. Jewry is still fearful of any too close relationships with Christendom; there is always a suspicion of a new-fangled missionary approach lurking under the surface; and the behaviour of the missionaries lends colour to the suspicion. Jews would argue that if they no longer say that "except you accept Jesus as Messiah you will be damned," but rather, "Is it not natural that we should wish to share with you the truth and happiness which we have found for ourselves?" the net result is the same. It is only the tactics which have changed.

In such circumstances, it is natural to say that the initiative must come from the side of the Christians, who are both a majority, and free from the fears and complexes that the tragic experience of millennia, culminating in the unparalleled horrors that have befallen this generation, have inevitably bred within Jewry. Christians would need to convince Jewry of their sincerity before they could expect a response, and even then they would need to be prepared for many rebuffs before Jews would really believe that Christians desired them to remain Jews, and were prepared on the religious plane to treat them as equals while they did so. That Jews and Christians can meet on the plane of common work for social and political betterment is already a step in the right direction; but it is no more than a step. And Jews know well that even this step has met the hostility and opposition of the Christian missionary societies.

The two other problems mentioned are both facets of the same problem—that of ensuring that ordinary Christian congregations, whether in church or Sunday school, are, in their ordinary worship and education, brought up automatically to accept the *attitude* that is the foundation of modern Biblical scholarship. It is not possible to rewrite the Bible; it is only possible to a limited extent to omit wholly from public use sections of the Bible which are repellent to modern Christian feeling—some of the early stories of the Bible and the imprecatory psalms are omitted in public worship, and Sunday school syllabi exercise a certain selectivity. What is wanted is something more fundamental, that congregations so instinctively recognise that they have in the Bible the interpretations of past generations that they will readily say to themselves that such or such was an interesting view beyond which we have to-day progressed; or that it is a pity that on such and such a point there was so much prejudice or misunderstanding in the mind of the writer. I am not excluding, of course, that there are other points on which a congregation might well wish that they had the faith and courage of the writers. But both will require a good deal more education from the pulpit—and in the pulpit—than is commonly the case to-day.

There will be some who will say that all this is too difficult and in any case would launch the Church on to a slippery slope from which it might be impossible to recover. It is much better to remain where we are. They are entitled to do so; but they must accept the reverse also of the picture. They must accept the ultimate responsibility for the massacres in Hitler's death-camps which are the result of the attitude they are unwilling to change. And they must accept that they are allies—however reluctantly—of the Fascism which is still alive and still making use of antisemitism.

For—let there be no mistake about it—even to-day, and even though very small sections of the Churches could be called actively antisemitic, the general influence of religious education, as it is now given, and of religious worship is to predispose those who share in it to view their Jewish neighbours with an unfriendly eye; and their Christian convictions form a well-watered seed-bed for the instillation of antisemitic prejudice from other sources. One hears too often from Jewish parents of their children coming home from school wondering why they have been called "Christ-killers" by their Protestant or Roman Catholic schoolfellows to be able lightly to dismiss the part that religious education plays in shaping in the youthful mind prejudices which will be dangerous when the child grows up.

The stage which is commonest among religious people to-day is a weak and dangerous compromise. It is probable that a majority of the members of the Protestant and Anglican congregations know vaguely that the doctrine of the verbal inspiration of the Scriptures is no longer held; that parts of the Bible are more primitive than others. But this vague belief is a very poor substitute for a new doctrine of the nature of inspiration. And in any case there is rarely any discrimination in the use of passages, emphasising wherein, if anywhere, the Church's doctrines have changed since the passage was written.

Meanwhile, there are several fields in which work can be done which will at least bring the Jewish and Christian communities into touch with each other and so help to remove those prejudices which arise directly from segregation and from ignorance. More than twenty-five years ago there was founded in London the first *Society of Jews and Christians* where members of the two faiths met to discuss matters of common interest on a basis of complete mutual respect. The Society is still a small body, but it is the only such group which openly discusses religious issues, and Jewish and Christian beliefs and practices, before a public forum. A little after the Society there was founded the *National Conference of Christians and Jews* in America, and in recent years a comparable Council has been set up in Great Britain. Other countries are slowly following suit. The common object of the *National Conference* and the comparable bodies in other countries is to provide a platform where Christians and Jews can meet to discuss and act on those questions of citizenship in which they have interests, and to which they can make contributions, because of their religious beliefs. But those beliefs themselves they do not discuss. The scope is more limited, the work done inevitably more superficial. The emphasis has to be laid so clearly on *common* tasks and ideas that the spiritual value of the differences tends to be minimised. But it is work of value as pioneering in the breaking down of ignorance and prejudice; and since their appeal is to the general public, it is at the moment important to get across to that public the fact that Jews and Christians share social and economic purposes and possess common social and economic doctrines of righteousness and service, and that these doctrines are very relevant to the community problems of to-day. Even if such be regarded as no more than the first steps towards the deeper understanding between the two religions, they are still first steps which far more people need to take over a far wider field than has yet been achieved in any country. And the sight of a Roman Catholic priest, a Protestant minister and a Jewish rabbi standing together on a single platform, urging a single message, is still a novelty, which in many countries would be a very effective answer to many of the allegations of the antisemites.

Parallel to the work of specific councils in which Jews and Christians meet by virtue of their religious affiliations are the community councils which take care that all the different sections of the citizenry are associated in communal purposes. Here Christians meet with Jews, not under that particular banner, but because Jews, with themselves and others, are concerned with the problems of betterment and all its ramifications which arise in our modern urban life. All such things can be good; for all can contribute to the removal of suspicion and ignorance.

There are also several fields in which Christians can share in the work of Jewish organisations. There are, both in America and in England, Christian Committees engaged in following and assisting the work of Palestine Jewry, both by making it better known and by providing a forum where visitors from Palestine can meet and discuss their problems with people who are interested and whom they might not naturally meet in Zionist offices. In the work of Jewish community councils and in the continuous struggle against defamation there is also a great deal of work that Christians can do. But when it comes to the fight with antisemitism, then Christians have no right to rest until they have taken the whole burden of this struggle off Jewish shoulders.

It cannot be said too often or too strongly that antisemitism is a Gentile, and pre-eminently a Christian, problem. It is not a Jewish problem, and to leave Jews to fight it is foolish as well as unjust. To-day the evidence should be enough to convince us that antisemitism is a highly organised political movement, which is used as a smoke screen by every kind of enemy, not merely of democratic and liberal thinking, but of everything which encourages the humane and generous instincts in mankind.

Nineteenth-century Europe invented this new technique, resting it firmly on ancient prejudices. At that time the United States were scarcely affected. To-day it is as true of America as it is of any other continent that antisemitism is an active and dangerous screen behind which the forces of reaction work with material and techniques which Nazism taught them and which did not cease to exist when Hitler fell.

The battle with antisemitism is the battle for decency and fellowship in communal life; and this is not a battle which concerns Jews only. Moreover, even if antisemitism were due to the faults of the Jews, which it is not, it would still be foolish for others to leave it to the Jews to fight alone, or even to take the leading part in the struggle. If a man has hypnotised himself into believing that the *Protocols of the Elders of Zion* are true, of what use is it for Jews to deny it? He expects them to deny it, and is conditioned to disbelieve any proofs they may adduce. But if he were a Roman Catholic and the denial came from his own Cardinal, an Episcopalian and it came from his Bishop, a Rotarian and it came from the central offices of Rotary, then there is some chance that it might have effect. Jewish defences are not only viewed with suspicion just in the quarters in which they are needed, but defences planned by Jews do often, in fact, misfire because they miss the best line of approach to the particular group concerned. There are Jewish problems with which Jews must deal, just as there are problems in every human group. That is work Gentiles cannot do for them. But antisemitism is a Gentile problem, pre-eminently a Christian problem, and it is time now that Christians and Gentiles realised that to pass resolutions of sympathy with its victims is a poor substitute for ensuring that the tale of its victims comes to an end. And, further, the work of the antisemites will not stop at the onslaught on Jewry. Jews are but the front-line troops, to be eliminated in order that the conquest of the citadel of the human soul and human decency may more easily be achieved.

We need to work at all these levels, both for the good they will do directly and because we have to realise that work at the deepest level will be slow to develop. It will be slow, not only because the changes which are needed cut deep into cherished views, but because what has been slowly built up over nearly two millennia cannot be broken down in a single generation. On the Christian side no fundamental change was possible until modern scholarship had opened a door to a new interpretation of the inspiration of the Scriptures; on the Jewish side we have to remember that the name of Jesus of Nazareth has stood for more than a thousand years of bitter and unjust persecution, that in that name Jews have been hounded from city to city, deprived of every right, and often compelled to surrender life itself. No people can easily obliterate such a memory.

That such changes will be accomplished slowly is no excuse for not taking the first steps now in this deepest field also. Rather it is an argument for doing so as soon as possible. Much would be achieved if there were more occasions on which Christian and Jewish scholars could meet to interpret their teaching to each other, and to discuss with mutual respect the foundations of their respective religions. More is needed than the speech of apologetic to a polite audience, whether made by the one side or the other. And more is possible in circles in which there is freedom to discuss, and recognition that neither side has divine authority for claiming the totality of truth—as well as the totality of common sense and intellectual honesty in its interpretation. More also is wanted than goodwill, though we do not have too much even of that. But the attitude that all religions are really the same, that differences do not matter, that what is required is goodwill, or tolerance, or any other cheerful panacea, is a danger and not an aid to real understanding. Differences do matter; they mean something. Intellectual honesty does matter; truth is not discoverable at will and without effort. Spiritual insight matters; for there are limits to the reach of intellect. There are times to be intolerant as well as times for tolerance. But there is a basis from which to work in the acceptance by each side of what history has objectively shown, that the two religions have grown up together; that the one has not replaced the other; that each can show in the lives of its adherents qualities of saintliness and the capacity to produce men of spiritual and moral worth, good citizens, good neighbours, good Jews and Christians. To-day Christians, like Jews, are minorities in modern society. It is not only in looking towards each other, but in together looking outwards towards the world, that the need for mutual understanding becomes most apparent.

It is well to hesitate before disturbing the beliefs of the ignorant devout, but we have hesitated already for so long that we have reversed the parable and made a fetish and an escape of safeguarding the one sheep who is safe, rather than of seeking the ninety and nine who are wandering in spiritual starvation in a world which is at once a vacuum and a torment. Modern man is the loneliest creature creation has ever known, and his powers of action are not stimulated but atrophied by the urgency and immensity of the task which confronts him.

Believing that to her alone was entrusted the task of guidance of the nations and the mantle of authority over them, the Church has made a pitiful failure of her commission. But what she failed to do alone it is still possible that Church and Synagogue can accomplish together. The Synagogue cannot take the first step; nor should she be expected to do so. Every day the Church delays, her confession both of guilt and of error adds to the difficulty, and reduces the strength available for the task. There is no past example to which to go back to seek enlightenment; but there are vast fields of riches to be explored, vast panoramas of opportunitity to be unfolded for those who have the courage to go forward.

Note.—In view of the attack made on the missions to the Jews, and in order to help the reader to form a balanced view by looking at the other side, I have given a list of books dealing with the missions, and with a certain number of individual converts, in the bibliographical note on this chapter.

CHAPTER SEVEN

THE RESPONSIBILITIES
AND OPPORTUNITIES OF JEWRY,
ESPECIALLY IN AMERICA

THE MASSACRE OF OVER six million Jews in Europe has done more than reduce the Jewish people to less than two-thirds of its pre-1939 numbers. It has entirely altered the balance of Jewry, and it closes an epoch of Jewish history. For the four centuries previous to this appalling destruction, the Jews of eastern Europe constituted from the three stand-points of religion, nationality and numbers the heart of the Jewish people. Prior to the great exodus to the new world and the west of Europe which followed the pogroms of 1881, more than two-thirds of the entire Jewish people lived in the stretch of land north and east of the Carpathians between the Baltic and the Black Sea. To-day that immense reservoir is, to all intents and purposes, empty.

It was within these territories that rabbinic Judaism was preserved and Jewish mysticism revived among the followers of the Besht. From eastern Europe until well on in the nineteenth century came the majority of the rabbis who served in western European communities. The decline which can be traced in orthodoxy, the narrowness and obscurantism of many communities, the prevalence of *pil-pul*, all owed their origin to conditions of life in those eastern communities. The superstition and escapism which so often accompanied the activities of the Chassidim had the same roots. The communities of the West might be more cultivated, the religion of the small Sephardic communities more cultured, but it was by the life in eastern Europe that Judaism had to be understood.

What is true of Judaism is equally true of the life of the Jews as a people. Even before formal emancipation set the seal on the movement of assimilation in the West, the smallness of the communities involved, the attractions of the western environments in which they lived, and the middle- and upper-class standards to which they were able to aspire, all tended to create a new type of Jew. He was not necessarily better or worse than the Jew of the eastern Pale. But in so far as he was different, he was different because of opportunities which were beyond the reach of the majority of his fellow Jews throughout the world. Thirty years ago, when western Europe had known nearly a century of emancipation, when the Jewry of the United States was already to be numbered by millions, more than half the Jews of the world still lacked civic and political equality with their non-Jewish neighbours. But, on the other hand, these Jews were still *a people*, as their western brethren had ceased to be. They were not a state, and they were not a race, but they were a people by all the stigmata by which one people is marked off from another. They had their own language and *mores*, their own dress and customs of food and conduct: they had their own law courts for civil cases, and above all, their own religion. In many of the cities in which they lived they formed the majority of the population; in others they formed at any rate the majority—usually the overwhelming majority—of the districts in which they lived. It was, if you like, a unique people, a people flung like a string of beads through the ghettoes and Jewish quarters of a thousand cities, towns and villages. But the beads were alike throughout the chain. A Jew who passed from the Jewish quarter of Vilna to that of Jassy, from that of Lodz to that of Odessa, found less difference in the life in his new quarters than he would have found passing from the Jewish to the Christian quarter of his own town.

From eastern Europe came the religious leadership; from eastern Europe came the Jewish masses who make up to-day the great Jewish communities of the new world; from eastern Europe came many of the scholars and scientists who in the last century have become famous in the intellectual life and universities of the West; in eastern Europe was born the political expression of the fact of Jewish nationhood; and from eastern Europe came the overwhelming majority of the first, as well as all subsequent, Aliyoth to Palestine. The Jewry of to-day has lost, not only one-third of its numbers, but its centre.

For to-morrow three separate, and very different, Jewish communities, though all of primarily eastern European origin, offer the possibility of becoming the new centre of Jewry—the communities of the U.S.A., the U.S.S.R., and of Palestine. We can understand the magnitude of the problem involved when we turn from such obvious facts as the terrible impoverishment of millions of Jews and their physical and psychological deterioration under years of appalling strain to the less obvious but equally important fact for the future that it is very difficult to see what is the effective bond of union between these three Jewries. Of common origin, their developments during the past generation have weakened, or even destroyed, their common interest. The Jew of the United States naturally thinks more of his relation to the American scene than of the fading memories—now largely inherited rather than personally experienced—of the Russian Pale. It is doubtful if the Jew of the Soviet Union distinguishes a Jew of the United States from any other citizen. He is merely another bourgeois, another capitalist, or another unfreed proletarian; while the Jew of Palestine is probably to him the willing or unwilling victim of British imperialism. And the Palestinian Jew, apart from the links with the outside world of organisation and finance, is fully occupied with problems in which the other Jewries are almost wholly inexperienced.

The community in the United States is unquestionably the largest, wealthiest and most influential Jewish community in the world to-day. To an increasing extent in the last twenty-five years it has taken the leading rôle in Jewish affairs throughout the world. It has interested itself in the life and problems of all other Jewries. Through the Joint Distribution Committee, it has been of incalculable service to Jews in need in all countries. At Versailles it provided much of the Jewish leadership; between the wars it was instrumental in founding and maintaining the World Jewish Congress. It has taken a similar lead in Zionist politics and finance. From 1945 onwards American Jewish money and personnel provided the motive power behind the underground lines across Europe to Palestine. In the religious field it is the centre of the Reform Movement, and its influence in liberal Judaism is as great as that of eastern Europe once was in the maintenance of Jewish orthodoxy.

The second greatest Jewish community of to-day is that of the U.S.S.R. In almost every respect, the picture it presents is the exact opposite to that of the U.S.A. Of the effective surviving communities, it is that which has been most shaken and changed by the cataclysm of the war. The facts about it are not easy to ascertain, but it appears to be true that about one-third of it was massacred by the Nazis; for the portions of the Soviet Union overrun by the Germans were those in which the overwhelming majority of the Jews lived. On the other hand, it may have gained between a quarter and half a million from the fugitives of the Nazi advance into Poland and the Baltic countries and the subsequent shifting of the Soviet frontier westward. The war uprooted it from the ancient centres of Jewish culture in which it had lived for centuries. Much of it to-day dwells east and south of the Urals, where no synagogue, no Yeshivah, has ever existed, and where no Jewish tradition lingers in the atmosphere. Its economic distribution leads to a belief that its survival as a separate community will be shortlived. Some half of the gainfully employed Jews before 1939 worked in employment which would lead them to prefer the language of the majority to Yiddish for the education of their children, and it is only as a Yiddish-speaking group that they are recognised as a separate nationality in the Union. The attempt to create a new Jewish republic in the east, in Biro-Bidjan, seems to have been a failure, though I have seen no reference to its development during or since the war.

It is not prejudiced to say that we cannot expect the Jewish population of the Soviet Union to play any large part in the battle of Jewry for survival, or to make any essentially Jewish contribution to the rebuilding of society outside its own frontiers. The social gospel of Communism has undoubtedly won the allegiance of the majority of the Jews of the U.S.S.R., though it is probably more difficult for a self-conscious Jewish community to accept the totalitarianism of the Soviet Government than for any other group within its borders. For there is nothing in the Jewish tradition which leads to the approval or acceptance of a society which condemns "deviation" or frowns on the widest freedom for the expression of different, or even contradictory, opinions on all subjects. What influence Jews may have in the future development of Soviet society it is impossible to say. They could scarcely participate in the kaleidoscope of world Jewish life except as a united "pressure group" for the particular ideology which they share with the other citizens of their country. But in the ideological battle they are not directly concerned as Jews or with Jews. On the other hand, it may well be that those Jews who remain in the countries within the Russian zone of influence may benefit from the success with which the Soviet authorities have fought their battle against antisemitism, and that the Jews of the Soviet Union may exercise their influence to see that the Jews of Poland and Rumania receive equal and proper treatment. But again we must wait for developments.

The third community is the Yishuv of Palestine. Very much smaller than either of the other two, its importance is not to be calculated by numbers, but by its ability to develop an autonomous and creative Jewish national and religious life, which is at the same time significant and influential for those Jewries still living in the Dispersion. In present conditions it is difficult to make prophecies as to its immediate political future, but this much at least can be said, that it will take some years to recover from the shocks of 1946 and 1947, and to absorb whatever number of newcomers it may be able to receive.

It is no disparagement of the creative work which has built up the vigorous community of the Yishuv to say that its shoulders are not yet broad enough to bear unaided the responsibility of providing the new centre of Jewish life. In the first place, the Jews of Palestine, including the Mizrachi and Agudah, have not yet begun to solve the problem of the place of religion in the national life. Indeed, the majority are only now beginning to be aware of the existence of the problem. It is to a large extent being brought home to ordinary Jews by their children, who find it difficult to limit their interest in the Bible to the strictly historical approach which they are often taught. But it is also an increasing concern of the thoughtful minority who are only too well aware of the spiritual maladies within the Yishuv, which owe their existence, not to the unceasing external struggle, but to that background of eastern Europe from which Zionism sets out to free its adherents. First, there is the effect on character of the restrictions under which the earlier settlers had lived in Tsarist Russia or in post-1919 Poland or Rumania. Secondly, they had no previous experience of political responsibility or the activities of a stable democracy. Thirdly—and this also is especially true of the earlier Aliyoth—they came largely, though not exclusively, from the generation which adopted rationalism or economic determinism as their alternative to the orthodoxy which they found untrue or unsatisfying. It was interesting to find that, "Do you believe in God?" often meant to Palestinian children: "Do you believe in the food laws?" Fourthly, there is in every settlement, office and factory a variety of background and language which does not make harmony and coherence easier. Lastly, we must remember that the whole Yishuv has known now ten years without real peace and that a considerable proportion of the immigrants of to-day have a background of terrible privation, outlawry and insecurity, with little knowledge of the calm delight of ordinary family life, with its variety of ages and interests within a balanced whole. "*Ich bin kein Mutters Kind. Ich bin ein Lagers Kind*" is true of thousands to-day and will be true of tens of thousands once Palestine receives the immigrants from Europe it is anxious to welcome. Facing all these facts, we can only marvel at the strength of the idealism which has upheld them, and the vigorous reality of the objective which they have set before themselves. For they have indeed wrought miracles. But they have not yet achieved stability or found that expression of their idealism which they can transmit to their children and succeeding generations.

Moreover, they are facing a political situation of quite exceptional complexity, with little help or guidance in their Jewish past as to the methods by which political problems can be approached and solved. They experience in especial measure the misfortune of all Jewry that rabbinic Judaism in its creative period had no opportunity of expressing in political life the fertile realism it showed in the realm of communal affairs and social responsibility. Their politics they have learned from the contemporary world; their parties and the list system by which their representatives are elected are a pure transference from the constitutions of post-1919 eastern Europe. In the countries of their origin they proved singularly incapable of constructing strong and effective democracies. I doubt if they have gained strength by a change of climate.

To these problems we must add the fact that the whole of Jewish life in Palestine is still in its formative period, and necessarily absorbed in its own problems, and that this will be intensified once any extensive immigration from post-war Europe takes place. For one must be under no illusion that the task of absorbing even one hundred thousand immigrants will be an easy one, or that the newcomers will instantly shake off all the psychological and physical strains produced by their experience in Europe during the war and, still more, during the years of bitterness and hopelessness which followed the "liberation" from the Nazis. And however much one may believe that political freedom is essential for the next stage of Jewish development, it would be very Utopian to believe that the responsibilities of independence will not bring in their train a thousand and one new problems whose solution will tax both leaders and people to the uttermost.

A review of the whole of the Jewish position in the modern world would naturally need to evaluate the position of the Jewries of many other countries. There are important communities in Great Britain and in the Dominions, and some of the communities of western Europe are rebuilding; two, in Switzerland and Sweden, are intact and played an honourable and generous rôle during the war. But while all these communities are important, and all make their contribution to the total picture, none could aspire to the position of leader and unifier of the Jews of the world. If, therefore, on the one hand, there can be no permanent new unity within Jewry which does not have the Yishuv near the centre of the picture, on the other hand, the responsibility of the Jewry of the Diaspora is still very great, and the main share in this responsibility will have to be taken by the Jewry of the United States.

There are three main fields in which the contribution of American Jewry will not merely be of paramount importance, but also quite irreplaceable for the foreseeable future.

The first is in the interpretation of the fact of nationhood in Jewish history. There will always be Jews living outside Palestine; and it is not easy to find the right expression of the communal tradition in Judaism in terms both of Palestine and of the life of an unsegregated minority in a democratic state. The state idea, as it determines the thinking of the Yishuv, may supplant rather than supplement the idea of a nation or people, as it is expressed in Jewish history. In the Diaspora the sharing of citizenship may lead only to those forms of assimilation which are self-destructive.

The second lies in the reinterpretation of Judaism in terms consistent at once with modern life and with the divine inspiration of Torah. The centre of Reform Judaism is unquestionably in the United States, but though the Reform movement is strong, its task is by no means completed, nor are its norms established. The same, of course, is true of modernised Christianity; and American Jews have therefore this advantage that they are sharing in the struggle for reinterpretation which is going on around them.

The third lies in the discovery of the place of Jewry ana of Judaism within the community of peoples and religions. Jews cannot live isolated from the world; they are part of a larger whole. From that larger whole they have a contribution to receive and to that larger whole they have, like all other peoples, a contribution to make. We must not be defeatist and accept antisemitism as a permanent factor in our society. But to-day antisemitism has made the making of the Jewish contribution exceptionally difficult. American Jews live in no ivory tower remote from experience of antisemitic activity, but in the struggle against it they are less isolated than many of their less fortunate brethren. Goodwill movements and the struggle for the expression of American democracy bring them valuable allies.

I am not pessimistic about the ability of American Jewry to rise to the height of the task demanded of it; but I would be no honest friend if I did not at the same time admit that much of its present situation fills me with misgiving.

There is no field in which these misgivings rise more quickly to the surface than in that which concerns the Jews as a people. The internecine conflict between the Zionists and the Assimilationists, the bitterness and unfairness often shown by the disputants, cannot but sadden anyone who knows how naturally and rightly these two movements spring out of Jewish history, and how complementary they are in the contribution they can make both to Jewish and to general life. Each is so justified in its positive attitude; each has forced itself by controversy to a denial which is so unjustified of the rightness of the other.

The spiritual vitality of Judaism, more than that of most other religions, owes much to the Jewish capacity for assimilation, which is totally different from the syncretism of, for example, Hinduism or Roman polytheism. All through Jewish history there has been an absorption of elements from the non-Jewish environment, from the early days when those Aramean groups, whose descendents were to become the Hebrew or Israelite people, were slowly developing a separate identity, through the Exiles right into medieval and modern times. No Jew thinks it disloyal to admit the influence of Persian ideas on post-exilic Judaism, of Hellenistic ideas on Philo, of Aristotle on Maimonides, of German philosophy on Moses Mendelssohn. Even the Christian environment in which Jewry lived for so many centuries was not wholly without influence, and in contemporary America the pastoral conception of the rabbinate as well as many communal Jewish activities owe something at least to the background of American Protestantism which the Jewish community has willingly assimilated. Assimilation only becomes something to deplore under two conditions, for only one of which Jews can be blamed. When there is not sufficient *Jewish* vitality in the Jewish community involved for its Judaism to digest that which it receives from outside, then the result, at one extreme, is a community like the Falashas of Abyssinia and, at the other, the Jewish adherents of Christian Science. This is indeed a purely internal Jewish affair; but Jews cannot be blamed when, as in nineteenth-century Europe, a Gentile interpretation of assimilation is dictated from outside as the basis of political or social recognition. In such conditions there is bound to be a steady stream of insincere "conversions" and a high proportion of mixed marriages, in which the Jewish partners only too willingly renounce any aspect of Judaism in married life and the upbringing of children. But in between these two extremes there is a wide field of honourable assimilation which makes no mean contribution to Jewish values, and which produces men of the type of Sir Moses or Claude Montefiore, or many of the leaders of the last and present generations of American Jewry. The sincerity of these British or American Assimilationists has brought both understanding and respect for Judaism in the Gentile environment in which they have lived, and yet left their Judaism untouched, because its foundations were sufficiently strong for them to approach and enjoy the world around them without fear that they would be seduced by it.

On the other hand, there is, historically, no question but that the Assimilationist is wrong in denying the persistence of the national idea throughout the whole of Jewish history, with the relatively small exception of a hundred years of the western world in which, as was explained in the fifth chapter, emancipation was offered on a false basis of individualism and a falsely created distinction between the religious and the communal idea in Jewish history. But even so the Assimilationist is right in seeing that the creation of a Jewish community or state in Palestine does not, of itself, provide a solution of the idea in the Diaspora, and might indeed be dangerously exploited.

Yet this is but to touch the fringes of the situation out of which Zionism was born. It is idle to blame it for taking the political forms which in the modern world are inseparable from such a movement; for the task which it legitimately set itself to perform could not be undertaken save by political means. The national life of Jews in eastern Europe was distorted, limited and depressed by conditions which they themselves could neither alter nor control. For this the Zionists desired to substitute a new national life lived under conditions of freedom; and this desire could but remain Utopian and escapist unless steps were taken to give political form and content to the ideal. Nor does the present political situation of Zionism, or the small part played in the up-building of Palestine by Jews with a consciously religious motive, alter the fact that Judaism itself was the motive force behind even the secularist Zionists, and to-day has much both to give to and to learn from the working out of a Jewish political life. For the very emphasis on community in Judaism lacks its final usefulness if it is unable to show what it can create in the highest form of community which is the autonomous political unit—I will not say the sovran state, for that idea is both purely Gentile and, in our present post-atomic age, outmoded. Though there have been a certain number of rabbis among the creators and leaders of the Zionist movement the fault lies with the Orthodox and not with the secularist that there is not more religious emphasis in Zionism. Yet even so the secularist Zionist is wrong if he denies that the bond which maintained the

Jewish nation in its hundreds of ghettoes was Judaism and nothing else. The religious and communal or national ideas in Jewish history are absolutely indistinguishable, and neither race, language nor any other criterion can be substituted for religion.

The basic cause of this futile and unhappy conflict is that both Zionist and Assimilationist tend to accept the Gentile idea of religion, of nation and of state. And this is the more unfortunate in that the modern world abundantly and tragically shows that the Gentile idea has proved pathetically inadequate to maintain society from attacks from within or without. The Christian division of spheres of interest between the religious and the secular authorities, reinforced as it was by the separation of Church and state which followed more than a hundred years of wars of religion, has meant that many of Europe's political concepts have been drawn from Germanic and Roman law and custom, and do not recognise the moral imperatives of prophetic Judaism. Personal morality and public morality have been regarded as two quite different things. The sphere of religion has been limited to man's personal standards and eternal destiny. Emancipated Jews were expected to limit their Judaism to the same concerns. With such a Judaism there was little tendency to interfere; but in all things concerned with public life, which were the affair of the state and not of the Church, the Jew was expected to accept the standards of the majority and was not invited to have ideas of his own. Moreover, at the epoch of emancipation the nation was not clearly distinguished from the state, and the corporate existence of separately organised nationalities within a single state was unimaginable—and it may be added that when in 1919 Europe tried to put it into practice it was also found to be unworkable. Confronted thus with a medley of ideas—a Christian conception of personal religion, a Roman or Germanic conception of a state, and a "modern" identification of state and nation (the idea stemmed from the French Revolution) the emancipated Jew can be forgiven for making mistakes. The conflict

GJa

was unexpected, and the solution not simple. But it rests on false premises, and its effect on Jewish life has been disastrous.

In this dual issue of Zionism and Assimilation American Jewry is in quite a special position. In the first place, assimilation is not, as it was in Europe, acceptance of a society whose whole ethos and *mores* have already been established, so that Jews have no other task than to mould themselves according to an already provided pattern. The whole of America is simultaneously assimilating what it means to be an American; and the new America which is evolving will not conform to any pattern laid down by any of the present American groups, not even the Roman Catholic, the Protestant or the Anglo-Saxon. One has only to think of the great coloured population to realise how long the road is which still stretches before the citizens of the U.S.A. before they have a single pattern to which future immigrants must automatically assimilate. But likewise America is in a most important position for developing, in company with the freedom-loving nations of the world, what it is to be what I have called an autonomous political unit in the world community. Her wealth, her numbers, the rich variety of her traditions could give her a predominant influence in the evolution of the new forms which the world is seeking. The Assimilationist in helping to build a nation should bring his own national idea to the structure; the nationalist or Zionist, if he cannot show his nationalism to contain something assimilable into the American landscape, impoverishes both America and his own national home.

At the present moment the conflict has been both bedevilled and distorted by circumstances in which the Assimilationist has some justification for accusing the Nationalist of an intolerable dualism of loyalty, and the Nationalist for accusing the Assimilationist of indifference to the fate of his co-religionists elsewhere. Both attitudes are the product of a sick society whose sickness cannot be blamed upon Jewry. In a world of nations equally seeking righteousness, the problem of dual loyalty would not arise.

To-day it does. To-day it can be argued that Zionist pressure groups in America or Britain are indifferent to the good or evil effects of their actions on British or American policy. The case is different from the dual loyalties of minorities in inter-war Europe, but to some the principle involved appears the same, and the consequence capable of being equally regrettable.

We must honestly face the fact that a resolution of the issue raised is not simple; perhaps even, in the present sick world, there is no solution which would do justice to both sides. But, if that is so, it is a case in which there should be more recognition by each side of the honesty and reasonableness of a difference of opinion, and on both sides a willingness to go as far as possible with the other. But again we have to recognise with sorrow that in a sick society it is unjustifiable to ask the member who has suffered most to show the sweet reasonableness we expect of the healthy.

But the problem of dual loyalty will still remain and needs to be faced. For myself, I would say that it was an attitude neither to be deprecated nor discouraged; and that all the political difficulties with which it may at any moment be surrounded can neither alter the basic truth that where a dual loyalty exists it rests upon the fact of an actual dualism in the person or group concerned, nor invalidate the desirability of maintaining and strengthening every genuine alternative passion which can reduce the exclusive monopoly of loyalty by the state of which each individual citizen is a member. It would be desirable rather to encourage multiple loyalties than to attack a dual loyalty, and it would also be more in accordance with the facts of our real situation in which the links that bind the world into groups by heredity, history, profession, religion or personal impulse, can only artificially be extended to, and confined by, the frontiers of our foolish sovranties.

The second great task of to-day is the reinterpretation of religion in terms comprehensible and socially creative to the common man of our day. This is a problem which Jewry shares with Christianity, and the problem presents itself to the two religions in almost identical terms. To understand it we need to distinguish between the maintenance power of a religion and its missionary or creative power. We must be honestly grateful that traditional orthodoxy, both Christian and Jewish, still presents a pattern which makes for noble living, and that many of the finest characters in the Christian and Jewish worlds are men and women who find complete spiritual satisfaction in the practice of their traditional faiths. It would be monstrous to deny that by their religious practices they come into contact with the living God. But when we look around us, we have with equal honesty to admit that the preaching of the traditional pattern of religion, even when it be both efficient and sincere, produces very little result upon the enormous majority of our contemporaries. They do not find that it provides a link between their daily lives and eternal truths; they do not find it relevant to the problems by which they are oppressed; and they are repelled by many secondary practices which are interwoven into the fabric of the traditional faiths and seem inseparable from them.

In this situation the emergence of reform groups was both right and inevitable. But I would say of the modernist movements of both Christianity and Judaism that they have not yet discovered the key to unlock the doors to the spiritual needs and inner life of modern man. Here I think that the failures of the two religions are different, but each can, perhaps, learn something from the other. Nothing better illustrates the weakness of the social gospel in the Christian tradition than the incurable habit of Christians in difficulty of going backwards. During the nineteenth century there arose, especially in the Anglo-Saxon world, a sane liberal movement which strove manfully to reinterpret the traditional faith in terms consonant with modern understanding, and with the revelations vouchsafed through the sciences, the scholarship and the discoveries of the last three hundred years. But there were weaknesses in this movement; in particular, it was unduly optimistic in its outlook on human progress. Things did not happen as the optimists expected; their analysis of the social and political environment proved faulty or shallow. And instantly Christians took fright. I remember the first rumblings of the cry "We must go back" in the conferences of the World's Student Christian Federation more than twenty years ago. By 1939 the retreat had become a rout. The panic rush to go backwards, to disavow any belief in the value of any revelation to, or discovery by, modern man assumed pathological proportions. The Roman Catholic developed a complex to return to Thomas Aquinas, the Lutheran became convinced that salvation was to be found in a return to Luther, the Calvinist to Calvin. Only the Anglicans were embarrassed by this nostalgia, which they felt in common with other Christians. For there is no sixteenth-century figure to whom they could return, save perhaps to the Great Queen herself. And, fortunately, Elizabeth did not indulge in the composition of theological tracts! To-day the whole Protestant world is hypnotised by the curious blend of obscurantism and inverted Utopian escapism which is associated with the name and writings of Karl Barth.

On the whole the movement in Judaism is less pronounced. This is, no doubt, partly due to the complexities which enshroud orthodoxy to those unfamiliar with it, and the restraints which it imposes on ordinary life. It is easier to change beliefs than build up a new set of daily habits and practices. In fact it would seem rather that within Reform Judaism there is danger of suffering from the opposite complaint—of not looking back enough. Rejecting the ceremonial laws and the divine authority of Torah and Talmud, some Reform Jews do not stop to enquire what lies behind the traditional beliefs, or gave rise to traditional practices. And so they are tempted to construct a belief for themselves, which owes less to anything traditionally Jewish than to contemporary non-Jewish religion, until their Judaism is indistinguishable from ethical culture or a unitarian Church. Now, to those who maintain that all religions are really the same, and that what matters are the things which we hold in common, this may appear a desirable development. I confess to setting a higher value on our differences, and to an unwillingness to sacrifice either that which is essentially Jewish or that which is essentially Christian for the sake of achieving a superficial and impotent unity. But there appear tendencies which go even further than this. There are those who, being unable to believe that God literally behaved in the way in which He is described in orthodox tradition, that He thundered from Sinai or spoke through the mouths of the prophets, reduce Him to a social convenience, a useful creation of the human mind for the sake of giving sanctity to certain difficult but socially desirable values. They see no difference between a theistic religion and an ethical society.

I am profoundly convinced that it is as true of Judaism as it is of Christianity that the peculiar quality which men seek in it, and by which in the last resort they judge it, is its ability to make real to men the existence of God and His relevance to their daily lives. No amount of pietism or social activities, whether among Jews or Christians, will compensate an inability to bring men to the living God. And here Judaism has a more difficult task than Christianity, for the Jewish tradition is weakest on its purely theological side. That which is not constantly used becomes rusty or brittle—this is as true of the sociology of Christians as of the theology of Jews. The Christians assumed that the religious man would act aright, and did not trouble continually to explore and to teach him the nature of right action. Judaism assumed that right-acting men would believe aright, and did not trouble continually to argue with them about the nature and activities of God.

I was interested in visiting the school at Ben Shemen in Palestine to find that 90 per cent. of the children said that they did not believe in God, but about the same percentage said that they did believe in "the Holy." Such can be the influence of the schoolmasters. For anything more pathetic than to substitute a vague belief in "the Holy," whatever that may be, for a belief in a living and acting God and Father, I find it difficult to imagine. It is natural for children to believe in God in a very concrete way. The difficult task, which neither Reform Jews nor indeed modernist Christians are meeting successfully, is to turn that childhood belief into an adult foundation of life. But until we can do it, we shall fail; and we shall fail all the more because the modern man does not find belief in God easy, and is far more in need of help than his primitive ancestor, who, in the midst of an unexplained world around him, would have found disbelief in a God both strange and frightening.

The other subject on which Reform Judaism does not appear fully to have found its feet arises from the situation during the period of emancipation to which I have already referred. It has shifted its emphasis so completely to individual morality that the social message of Judaism as something to be communally worked out and endorsed is lost. I have read pronouncements of Reform rabbis on political issues which differ in no way from those of any Protestant pulpit. They were purely individual expressions of belief. But a Judaism which has not a corporate conviction about the moral use of the political responsibility of a citizen in a democratic country has almost ceased to be Judaism. It is easy to retain the noble generalisations of the prophetic period; but the essential historical fact about Judaism is that it was not until the rabbis had taken these noble generalisations and unravelled them thread by thread into an application to all the concrete issues of daily life that they actually began to work. To take an example from the deepest theological issues: it was the rabbis, not the prophets, who coped with idolatry among Israelites. I believe it is right to say that the Torah tells us how men, in their generation, rightly interpreted the will of God revealed to them; that the Talmud carried on this interpretation at a later stage. But circumstances have changed since then, and a new interpretation is needed. But it is spiritual and intellectual poverty to substitute for the corporate expression of the will of God in the Torah or Talmud the personal predilections of the individual rabbi.

Here we come to the bridge between my second problem

—the reinterpretation of Judaism—and my third, the discovery of the place of Jewry and Judaism within the community of peoples and religions. In a previous chapter I described Judaism as a combination of non-cosmopolitan universalism and non-exclusive particularism. If that description is a fair one, then the reinterpretation of Judaism is inextricably interwoven with the destiny of the Jewish people, whether we consider the life of a Jewish community, living as a minority in a non-Jewish state, or whether we consider the political problems which will confront a free Jewish community in Palestine. In both cases there is a need, a great and immediate need, to rediscover and to evolve from (for it needs both) the message which is found at its clearest in the prophets rather than the later rabbinic writings. The European conceptions of both state and Church are not Jewish, and the Jew is never wholly at home within them, save by surrendering vital parts of his Jewish inheritance. But to fit the Jewish conception of the political and religious community into the life of to-day is not easy. A Palestine attempting to enforce on all citizens the orthodoxy of the Shulhan Aruch would be as intolerable as a Jewish community in the Diaspora acting as a united pressure group on all political issues at the dictates of a rabbinical council. We cannot restore the past integrally; but we cannot abandon it either. For the political activity of the prophets was something of immense moral importance in the developing of human society, and we have not progressed, but gone backward in many respects since their day.

I have stressed the prophets, because they were speaking to a free nation, and constantly dealing with the highest political and national issues, whereas by the time of the rabbis Judæa had already lost its political freedom. But, so far as method is concerned, it is more to the rabbinical than to the prophetic period that we need to turn. For it is not a question to-day of finding a new series of outspoken preachers and writers. We have that. It is a question of finding a method by which a community, in its examination and solution of its everyday political problems, can be constantly brought into touch with fundamental conceptions of basic morality and communal righteousness, and consciously seek to embody these in the policies which it adopts and by which it intends to live.

There are many departments of life in which men have given practical effect to their realisation that the modern world is so complex that we can no longer produce men like Maimonides or Thomas Aquinas, who took all knowledge as their sphere, and appeared to their contemporaries to know all that could be known. We are just beginning to rediscover that there is such a thing as a group mind, and that it can be broader, deeper, and wiser than the mind of an individual, or even than the total of the minds composing it, considered separately. There was a time when Judaism could produce this group mind in religion, while still preserving both flexibility and the possibility of disagreement. To-day we leave the field to scientific, industrial and technical institutes. To-day Jews are apt to be proud that *quot Judaei, tot sententiae*, and they are perhaps more divided and more individualistic than any comparable group. That does not alter the fact that Judaism, historically considered, possesses the strongest of all communal traditions, and the most practical experience of how the group mind can be fostered. Sooner or later we will have to realise that we need to explore the creation of group thinking in the fields of social and political morality; and the state of the world certainly suggests that the sooner we do it the better. And a Christian might ask: if Jews think it difficult for themselves, do they find evidence in the Christian world that Christians would succeed better at the task?

There is no question but that a free Jewish community in Palestine would have to be a very special community. The external conditions of its life in the midst of an Arab world whose permanent hostility would be irredeemably fatal to its very existence secure that. By none of the normal means of power politics, or of playing off one group against another, could it survive. It will survive only by finding a new way of life, a way of life which gradually wins for it the recognition and acceptance of its neighbours. But equally particular is the position of a Jewish community in the Diaspora. If it is to be truly Jewish it cannot avoid a feeling of both interest and responsibility in all the problems of its social and political environment. But, living as it does with the perpetual danger of antisemitic misrepresentation of its interest, it needs, far more than do the Christian Churches, which are exposed to the danger only of being ignored, to discover exactly the right form for its interest and its responsibility to take.

I believe that what is needed for both the Palestinian and the Diaspora situations is some kind of Jewish institute of politics, transferring into modern form the rabbinical academies of the Gaonic epoch. It may be argued that there are plenty of institutes of politics, and that for the Jews to create one of their own would merely emphasise separatism in a field in which close co-operation with non-Jewish enterprises is both possible and desirable. There is much force in this argument, and there is only one ground on which it would be legitimate to set it aside—that the foundations on which such an institute would work are basically different. But that argument is, I believe, valid. The scientific institutions of to-day are purely humanistic. They know only one "reality"—man—and they pride themselves on having no *a priori* hypotheses in their examination of man and his activities. They are concerned with what man does, not with value judgments about what he ought to do. And there is ample evidence that work of extreme importance can be and is done along such lines. But for Jews, as also for Christians, there are two "realities," man and God. And for them God, and His power as well as His purpose, is a reality as objectively related to human life as is man himself. A Jewish institute of politics *would* start with *a priori* judgments. It would not, like the academies of Babylon, be bound by the written word of Torah, and confine its task to interpretation. But it would start with the belief in the primacy of moral values, in an "ought" as well as an "is" in human affairs, and in the power of God working for righteousness.

The authority of such an institute would be a moral and not a coercive authority. It would rest on the integrity and intelligence of the men who composed it, and not on the power to excommunicate. But a moral authority would be adequate to its purpose and its influence might be felt outside as well as within the Jewish communities of the world. In a number of countries I am convinced that it could count on the most sympathetic co-operation in Christian circles and possess a wide power for good in the life of the nation. It could likewise serve to bring realism to much Utopian religious feeling to-day, among Jews as well as among Christians. And it would greatly strengthen, deepen, and add much wisdom to the relations between Diaspora Jewry and Palestine. Pressure and propaganda will not solve the political dilemma in that now unhappy country. Real study and understanding may still work miracles.

Mankind is entering a new age. Society is taking new forms and is confronted with new problems. At the moment men are so fascinated with, or so terrified by, the immense scientific advance of the past century, and particularly by the discovery of atomic energy, that religion seems to most but a comfortable backwater; but let us not forget that the fault has largely lain with our religious leaders, whether we think of Christianity or of Judaism. And it is certainly true that it lies with us who believe in God to regain our contact with the world around us, for the world will not make the first advance. May it not be said by our generation that we have shut up the Kingdom of Heaven against men, when it was our task, both by our lives and our teaching, to reveal it.

BIBLIOGRAPHIES

T H E N A T U R E O F T H I S book results in only certain chapters being susceptible to bibliographical treatment. I shall not attempt to give a list of books for the first chapter or the last. Likewise, on the other chapters I shall not give the general histories which inevitably form a background for specialist reading, but only a selection of the specialist studies themselves.

Chapter Two

The work of resetting Jesus in his Jewish background has been undertaken by many scholars, Jewish as well as Christian, during the last twenty-five years. Naturally, the books listed will not all present the same point of view, or appear to any single reader equally objective. The most complete examination of the references to the contacts of Jesus with the Pharisees will be found in the book of Riddle, but the thesis which the book itself develops seems to me an outstanding example of the impossibility of writing history on the basis of the current school of form criticism.

I. Abrahams. *Studies in Pharisaism and the Gospels.* 1st and 2nd Series. Cambridge, 1917 and 1924.

B. H. Branscomb. *Jesus and the Law of Moses.* Richard R. Smith, 1930.

H. G. Enelow. *A Jewish View of Jesus.* Bloch Pub. Co. 1931.

J. Klausner. *Jesus of Nazareth, His Life, Times and Teaching.* Macmillan Co., New York, 1929.

T. W. Manson. *The Teaching of Jesus.* Cambridge, 1931.

C. G. Montefiore. *The Synoptic Gospels.* 2 vols. 2nd Ed. Macmillan, London, 1927.

C. G. Montefiore. *Rabbinic Literature and Gospel Teachings.* Macmillan, London, 1930.

Max Radin. *The Trial of Jesus of Nazareth.* University of Chicago Press, 1931.

James Parkes. *Jesus, Paul and the Jews.* Student Christian Movement Press, 1936.

D. W. Riddle. *Jesus and the Pharisees. A Study in the Christian Tradition.* University of Chicago Press, 1928.

E. R. Trattner. *As a Jew sees Jesus.* Scribners, 1931.

Thomas Walker. *What Jesus Read; His Dependence and Independence.* Allen and Unwin, 1925.

Thomas Walker. *Jewish Views of Jesus; an Introduction and an Appreciation.* Allen and Unwin, 1931.
S. Zeitlin. *Who Crucified Jesus?* Harper, 1942.

Many books have now been written on the Judaism of this period, and the following list to some extent serves both this and the following chapter. Attention has been concentrated mainly on the Pharisees, but the work of Oesterley contains an invaluable survey of the various Jewish sects during the period. There is now a considerable literature dealing with apocalyptic, and most of the texts have been published by the S.P.C.K. of London in the series of Palestinian Jewish texts. Works definitely dealing with the relations of Judaism to early Christianity are listed in the bibliography of the following chapter.

Edwyn Bevan. *Jerusalem under the High Priests.* Arnold, 1912.
Ben Zion Bokser. *Pharisaic Judaism in Transition.* Bloch, 1935.
L. Finkelstein. *The Pharisees.* 2 vols. Jewish Publication Society of America, 1938.
R. Travers Herford. *The Pharisees.* Macmillan Co., New York, 1924.
J. Z. Lauterbach. *The Pharisees and Their Teaching.* Bloch, 1930.
R. Leszynsky. *Die Sadduzäer.* Berlin, 1912.
G. Foot Moore. *Judaism in the First Centuries of the Christian Era.* 3 vols. Harvard University Press, 1927.
W. O. E. Oesterley. *The Jews and Judaism during the Greek Period.* S.P.C.K., 1942.
Emil Schürer. *A History of the Jewish People in the Time of Jesus Christ.* 5 vols. English translation. Edinburgh, 1896.

Chapter Three

No attempt has been made to list commentaries on different Pauline letters, or general works on the theology of Paul. Such can be found in any theological library.

M. Friedländer. *Patristische und Talmudische Studien.* Vienna, 1878. *Zur Enstehungsgeschichte des Christenthums.* Vienna, 1894. *Synagoge und Kirche in ihren Anfängen.* Berlin, 1908.
E. Travers Herford. *Christianity in Talmud and Midrash.* Williams and Norgate, London, 1903.
G. Hoennicke. *Das Judenchristenthum.* Berlin, 1908.
Foakes Jackson and Kirsopp Lake. *The Beginnings of Christianity. Part One; The Acts of the Apostles.* 5 vols. Macmillan, 1920–33.
G. Kittel. *Die Probleme des Palästinischen Spatjudentums und das Urchristenthum.* Stuttgart, 1926.
J. Klausner. *From Jesus to Paul.* Allen and Unwin, 1943.

W. L. Knox. *St. Paul and the Church of Jerusalem*. Cambridge, 1925.

Kaufmann Kohler. *The Origins of the Synagogue and the Church.* Macmillan, 1929.

C. G. Montefiore. *Judaism and St. Paul*. Max Goschen, 1914. (There are, in addition, several articles of Dr. Montefiore scattered through the *Jewish Quarterly Review*, First Series.)

W. O. E. Oesterley. *The Jewish Background of the Christian Liturgy*. Oxford, 1925.

James Parkes. *Jesus, Paul and the Jews*. Student Christian Movement Press, 1936.

C. H. Rendall. *The Epistle of St. James and Judaic Christianity*. Cambridge, 1927.

H. L. Strack. *Jesus, Die Haeretiker und die Christen nach den ältesten jüdischen Angaben*. Leipzig, 1910.

Chapters Four and Five

I have not listed books which, while dealing with the subject, yet, in my opinion, exhibit definite prejudice leading to misrepresentation of the facts. Such an exclusion rejects not merely the semi-scholarly products of the Jewish Research Institute of Nazi Germany, but also a good deal of the work written from specifically Christian missionary standpoints. Such books are not reliable, and are curious evidence in themselves of the strange products of the missionary attitude referred to in Chapter Six. An exception (in that I have mentioned it) is the *Adversus Judaeos* of Lukyn Williams, a work which, because of its scope, cannot be omitted, but in which the admirable scholarship of its author is continually compromised by his point of view. The omission of these books naturally does not mean the exclusion of books written by devout members of both the Roman Catholic and of Protestant Churches; for I include works of such men as Coudenhove Kalergi and Moehlman.

M. I. Bedarride. *Du Prosélytisme et de la Liberté Religieuse*. Paris, 1875.

J. Bergmann. *Jüdische Apologetik in neutestamentlichen Zeitalter*. Berlin, 1908.

H. Coudenhove Kalergi. *Anti-Semitism throughout the Ages*. Edited and brought up to date. Hutchinson, 1935.

B. Blumenkranz. *Die Judenpredikt Augustins*. Basle, 1946.

S. Grayzel. *The Church and the Jews of the Thirteenth Century*. Dropsie College, Philadelphia, 1933.

M. Güdemann. *Jüdische Apologetic*. Glogau, 1906.

J. Guttmann. *Die Scholastik des Dreizehnten Jahrhunderts*. Breslau, 1902.

B. Lazare. *L'Antisemitisme; Son Histoire et ses Causes.* Paris, 1894.

M. Lifschitz-Golden. *Les Juifs dans la Littérature Française du Moyen Age.* Columbia University, 1935.

M. Mieses. *Der Ursprung des Judenhasses.* Harz Verlag, 1923.

C. H. Moehlman. *The Christian-Jewish Tragedy. A Study in Religious Prejudice.* Rochester, 1933.

L. I. Newman. *Jewish Influence on Christian Reform Movements.* Columbia University Press, 1925.

James Parkes. *The Jew and His Neighbour.* Student Christian Movement Press, 1938. *The Conflict of the Church and the Synagogue.* Soncino Press, 1934. *The Jew in the Medieval Community,* Soncino Press, 1938. *The Jewish Problem in the Modern World.* Home University Library, Oxford University Press, New York, 1946.

H. Pflaum. *Die Religiose Disputation in der Europaischen Dichtung des Mittelalters.* Geneva, 1935.

H. J. Schoeps. *Jüdisch-Christliches Religiongespräch in 19. Jahrhunderten.* Berlin, 1937.

M. Stern. *Stellung der Päpste zu den Juden.* Kiel, 1893.

J. Trachtenberg. *The Devil and the Jew; the Medieval Conception of the Jew and Its Relation to Modern Antisemitism.* Yale, 1943.

Hugo Valentin. *Antisemitism.* V. Gollancz, 1936.

A. M. Lukyn Williams. *Adversus Judaeos; A Bird's-eye View of Christian Apologiae until the Renaissance.* Cambridge, 1935.

I. M. Wise. *A Defence of Judaism against Proselytising Christianity.* Cincinnati, 1889.

Chapter Six

In order that the reader may not think either that those who conduct missions to the Jews are themselves charlatans, or that the converts from Judaism to Christianity contain no men of the highest integrity and noblest character, some books dealing with the subject are listed here. I have omitted books written from the missionary standpoint which, in their prejudice, approximate to the medieval attitude or to that of secularist modern antisemitism. I have also included one curious tract on the Jewish treatment to which some converts at least have been subjected.

Anon. *The Conversion and Persecution of Eve Cohan now called Elizabeth Verboon, a Person of Quality of the Jewish Religion.* London, 1680.

J. Bonsirven. *Juifs et Chrétiens.* Paris, 1936.

J. F. A. de Le Roi. *Geschichte der Evangelischen Juden-mission.* 2 vols. Leipzig, 1899. *M. S. Alexander, Evangelische Bischoff v. Jerusalem.* Leipzig, 1897. *Isaak da Costa; der Hollandische Christ und Dichte aus Israel.* Leipzig, 1899.

K. Hoffman. *Ursprung und Anfangstätigkeit des ersten päpstlichen Missionsinstitut.* Munster, 1923.

Julius Richter. *A History of the Prostestant Missions in the Near East.* Edinburgh, 1910.

J. Wilkinson. *Israel My Glory.* London, Mildmay Mission, 1889.

Joseph Wolff. Various journals on his travels in the East.

Books dealing with the "Goodwill Approach"

N. D. Baker, C. J. H. Hayes, and R. W. Strauss. *The American Way. A Study of Human Relations among Catholics, Protestants and Jews.* Willett, Clarke and Co., New York, 1936.

E. R. Clinchy. *All in the Name of God.* John Day Co., New York, 1934.

Lev Gillet. *Communion in the Messiah.* Lutterworth Press, 1942.

M. Lazaron. *Common Ground; A Plea for Intelligent Americanism.* Liveright, 1938.

H. F. Rall and S. S. Cohen. *Christianity and Judaism compare Notes.* Macmillan, New York, 1927.

C. E. Silcox and Galen M. Fisher. *Catholics, Jews and Protestants; A Study of Relationships in the United States and Canada.* Harper, 1934.

W. W. Simpson. *Jews and Christians To-day.* Epworth Press, 1940.

G. A. Yates (edited by). *In Spirit and in Truth; Aspects of Judaism and Christianity.* Hodder and Stoughton, 1934.

NOTES

Chapter One: Judaism and Christianity in the Purpose of God

1. See *The History of Israel* (Oxford, 1932), Vol. I, pp. 80 and 88 *ff.*, and *Hebrew Religion: Its Origin and Development* (London, 1930), pp. 156 *ff.*

2. *Briefe v. Franz Rosenzweig.* Ed. E. Rosenzweig, Schocken Verlag, 1935. See the article of Dr. A. Altmann in the *Journal of Religion*, 1944.

3. Rotapfel Verlag, Zurich u. Leipzig, 1922. Victor Gollancz has, since this was written, published Ragaz' *Israel, Judaism and Christianity*.

4. Exod. xix. 8 and xxiv. 3.

5. The name given to the scholars who produced the Mishna—roughly the period from 70–200 C.E.

6. E.g. "The Torah is not in Heaven: we pay no heed to a Bat Kol." See following note.

7. See article "Bat Kol" in *Jewish Encyclopædia*.

8. *Essays on Zionism and Judaism*, tr. Leon Simon, London, 1922. Essay on Judaism and the Gospels.

9. Isa. xlii. 1–4, xlix. 1–6, l. 4–9, lii. 13–liii. 12.

10. Job xlii. 2, 3, 5, 6.

11. 1 Cor. iv. 10. For Paul's career, see the following verses and 2 Cor. xi. 24–30.

Chapter Two: The Relations of Jesus with the Judaism of His Day

1. Luke i. 1–4.

2. Luke iii. 7–8.

3. Matt. iii. 7.

4. Mark ii. 1–12.

5. Luke v. 21.

6. Matt. ix. 3.

7. John ii. 13, v. 1, vi. 4, vii. 2, x. 22, xi. 55.

8. *Readings in St. John's Gospel*, I, pp. xi *ff.* and 105 *ff.*

9. John v. 15–16, vii. 2, etc.

10. John xviii. 3.

11. Mark vi. 1–6.

12. Luke iv. 16–30.

13. See *The Origin of the Gospel according to St. Matthew*, G. D. Kilpatrick, Oxford, 1946.

14. Mark i. 22.

15. *Ibid.*, 23–6.

16. *Ibid.*, 27–8

17. *Ibid.*, 44.

18. Mark ii. 14–17.

19. *Ibid.*, 23 and iii. 1–2.

20. Mark x. 19.

21. Mark xii. 28–31.

22. Matt. xxiii. 23; Luke xi. 42.

23. Matt. v. 17–19 and xxiii. 2f.

24. Luke xvi. 18.

25. Matt. v. 32 and xix. 9.

26. Matt. iii. 2; Mark i. 15.

27. Matt. vi. 33.

28. Matt. v. 29–30, 40, 41.

29. Mark ii. 27.

30. Rom. xiii. 8–10.

31. Jer. xliv. 15–19.
32. Mark iii. 22.
33. See article on "Hypocrisy" in *Jewish Encyclopædia*.
34. See the demands for silence about healings, Mark i. 44, iii. 12, v. 43, etc.
35. E.g. John iii. 13–16, to Nicodemus; iii. 31, witness of John Baptist; iv. 10 and 26, to the Samaritan woman; and publicly from v. 17 onwards.
36. E.g. Mark viii. 30.
37. Luke xiii. 31.
38. Mark iii. 6.
39. John vi. 15.
40. *Who Crucified Jesus?*, Solomon Zeitlin, New York, Harpers, 1942.
41. Acts iv. 5, v. 17, xxii. 30.
42. Matt. xxvii. 25.
43. Luke xxiii. 34.
44. Zech. ix. 9.
45. See *Christianity in Talmud and Midrash*, Travers Herford, pp. 78 *ff.*
46. Acts i. 6.

Chapter Three: Paul and the Foundation of the Christian Church

1. Acts ii. 23, iii. 17, 18.
2. Acts. i. 6 *ff.*
3. Acts iii. 1 *ff.*
4. Acts iv. 1 *ff.*
5. Acts v. 15, 16.
6. *Ibid.*, 17–21.
7. *Ibid.*, 34–9.
8. Acts vi. 14.
9. Acts viii. 3.
10. Acts xxii. 3.
11. In the *Clementine Recognitions* it is suggested that Paul believed Peter had fled to Damascus. See *The Jew of Tarsus*, Hugh Schonfield, Macdonald, 1946, pp. 87 *f.*
12. See C. G. Montefiore, *Judaism and St. Paul*, p. 117, etc.
13. Acts xi. 18.
14. *Ibid.*, 22–5.
15. Acts ix. 27.
16. Gal. ii. 7.
17. Acts xv, 1 and 5; Gal. vi. 12.
18. Cf. *The Doctrine of the Last Things*, W. O. E. Oesterley, London, 1909, for the variety of views existing.
19. Acts xv. 19–20. That these regulations were originally the Noachian Commandments has been suggested by both Jewish and Christian scholars since the Middle Ages. On the Noachian Commandments, see the *Jewish Encyclopædia*.
20. Galatians, *passim*.
21. Acts xiii. 46 and xviii. 6.
22. Acts xiv. 1 and xviii. 19.
23. Acts xx. 22–4.
24. Acts xxi. 17 *f.*
25. *Ibid.*, 21.
26. *Ibid.*, 23, 24, 26.
27. *Ibid.*, 27–8.
28. Acts xxii. 3.
29. Acts xxiii. 2.
30. *Ibid.*, 6.
31. *Ibid.*, 9.

32. Acts xxiv. 5, 6.
33. *Ibid.*, 14.
34. Acts xxv. 8.
35. *Ibid.*, 20.
36. Acts xxvi. 4–7.
37. *Ibid.*, 32.
38. Acts xxviii. 17.
39. *Peake's Commentary on the Bible*, p. 800.
40. *Acts of the Apostles*, R. B. Rackham, Westminster Commentaries, p. 430.
41. E.g. 1 Cor. xii. 12, 27; Eph. iv. 1–15.
42. Oesterley, *The Jews and Judaism during the Greek Period*, p. 148.
43. Cf. *The Conflict of the Church and the Synagogue*, J. Parkes, Soncino Press, 1934, p. 116.
44. Vergil, *Æneid*, vi, 314: *tendebant manus ripae ulterioris amore.*
45. Acts xviii. 6.
46. *Ibid.*, 11.
47. 1 Cor. i. 11.
48. *Ibid.*, 12 *ff.*
49. 1 Cor. v. 1–2, etc.
50. 1 Corinthians, from Chap. vi onwards.
51. Matt. iii. 9.
52. Acts xiii. 39; from Paul's sermon at the Pisidian Antioch.
53. Jas. ii. 14 *ff.*
54. Cf. Rom. iv; Gal. iii. 6.
55. Article 13. The articles of the Anglican Church were originally drawn up in 1562. They are appended to the Book of Common Prayer and still have to be read publicly and "generally assented to" by every priest on entering into charge of a parish.
56. Rom. vii. 12.
57. Gal. iii. 24.
58. Jer. xxxi. 33.
59. Gal. iii. 10.
60. Gal. v. 3.
61. 2 Cor. iii. 7.
62. Rom. x. 3.
63. Rom. xi. 25.
64. Gal. iii. 20.
65. Col. ii. 9.
66. 1 Cor. xii. 13; Gal. iii. 28.
67. From the Anglican Catechism. Answers 2 and 17.
68. Cassiodorus, *Varia*, ii. 27. Pat. Lat. LXIX, c. 561.
69. Mark vii. 15.
70. Mark vii. 19.
71. Matt. xxiii. 23.
72. Matt. v. 18.
73. *Dialogue*, Chap. XLVII.
74. *The Conflict*, pp. 128 *ff.* and 402 *ff.*
75. Eusebius, *Eccl. Hist.*, II, xxiii.
76. *The Conflict*, pp. 79 *f.*
77. *Ibid.*, p. 86.

Chapter Four: The Traditional Attitude of Christianity to Judaism

1. Agobard, *Ep. ad Nibridium Ep. Narbonensem*, c. 113. Quoted in *Jew in Medieval Community*, J. Parkes, p. 30.
2. See *Conflict of Church and Synagogue*, J. Parkes, pp. 95, 172, 303.
3. Anastasius of Sinai, *Disputatio contra Judaeos, III. The Conflict*, pp. 281 *f.*
4. Jacob of Serug, *First Homily against the Jews*, line 283. *The Conflict*, p. 99.

5. *Profession of Faith of Church of Constantinople. The Conflict*, p. 397.
6. Cf. *History of the Jews in England*, C. Roth, Oxford, 1941, Chap. VII.
7. See *The Conflict*, p. 163.
8. *Ibid.*, p. 161.
9. *Ibid.*, p. 102, and see General Index, *Apocryphal New Testament*.
10. Epiphanius, *Heresies*, xiv–xx, xxix, xxx, liii.
11. Justin, *Trypho*, Chap. XIII.
12. Ps. Cyprian, *Adv. Judaeos* in *Corpus Scriptorum Ecc. Lat.*, III, iii, p. 135.
13. Cod. Theod., XVI, viii, 1.
14. Cod. Theod., *Nov.* 3.
15. The *Henoticon* of the Emperor Zeno (474–91), quoted in Michael the Syrian, *Chron.*, Bk. ix, Chap. VI, says that "thousands have perished in the massacres and not only the earth but the air is contaminated with blood."
16. Cod. Theod., VII, viii, 2; XVI, viii, 12, etc. See *The Conflict*, App. 1, 2, p. 391.
17. See Ambrose, Ep. xl and xli.
18. *The Conflict*, pp. 276 *ff.*
19. *Ibid.*, p. 293.
20. Told with a wealth of detail by the chronicler, George Hamartolus. Bk. iv, Chap. 248, in Pat. Graec., CX, c. 916.
21. *The Conflict*, p. 109.
22. See *According to the Hebrews*, Hugh Schonfield.
23. *The Conflict*, pp. 118 *ff*. 189 *ff*. 305 *ff*. and 342 *ff*.
24. Charter of King John of France, 1361: "[les juifs] n'ont pais ne lieu propre aucun en toute Chrétianité, ou ils puissent demourer fréquenter ne y habiter se ce n'est de la propre et pure licence et volonté du Seigneur ou Seigneurs soubz qui il se voudroient asseoir pour demourer soubz euls comme leur subgiez, et qui à ce les voudroient recueiller et recevoir."
25. Trachtenberg, *The Devil and the Jew*, p. 12.
26. *Le Scorpion symbole du Peuple juif*, M. Bulard, Paris, 1935.
27. See *The Life and Miracles of St. William of Norwich*, by Thomas of Monmouth. Ed. by A. Jessopp and M. R. James, Cambridge, 1896.
28. Lukyn Williams, *Adversus Judaeos*, pp. 228 *ff*.
29. *Ibid.*, pp. 245 *ff*.
30. *The Conflict*, pp. 285 *ff*., 290.
31. *Histoire des Juifs de France*, L. Berman, Paris, 1937, pp. 101 *f*.
32. *Vineam Sorac* of August 4th, 1278.
33. Under the title *Alteca Boteka* (Al Tehi ka-Abotekha).
34. Collected in *Die päpstlichen Bullen über die Blutbeschuldigung*, Munich, 1900.
35. The badge at the Fourth Lateran Council, 1215; segregation at the third Lateran 1179; the conversional sermon, Nicholas III, 1278; burning of books, Béziers, 1255.
36. See *Die Juden in der Karikatur*, E. Fuchs, Munich, 1921.

Chapter Five: The Rediscovery that Jews are a Living People and Judaism a Living Religion

1. See *J. Bodin u. seine Beziehung zum Judentum*, J. Guttmann, in *Monatschrift z. Geschichte u. Wissenschaft des Judentums*, XLIX.
2. See *Martin Luther: Schriften wider Juden und Turken*, Munich, 1936.
3. *Synagoga Judaica*, Ed. 1641, Chap. 36, p. 465.
4. *Lightfoot's Works*. First Ed., Vol. I, p. 997. *Miscellanies*, Chap. 7.
5. *Ibid.*, p. 376. *Parergon concerning the Fall of Jerusalem*, Section 12.
6. Introduction to Vol. I: pages beginning "*habuerunt aetates*" and "*suis propinant.*"   , p. 18.
7. *Dissertatio*
8. *The Four Degenerate Sons*, pp. 337 *ff*.

9. *Tractatus de Juribus Judaeorum*, Chap. i.
10. *Nazarenus*, Appendix, pp. 2 and 8.
11. *Jüdische Merckwuerdigkeiten*, pp. 92 *ff*.
12. Basnage, English trs., pp. iii and iv.
13. *Ibid.*, Bk. VI, Chap. i, par. 4, Ed. 1706.
14. *Essai sur la Régeneration physique, morale, et politique des Juifs*, pp. 193 *f*.
15. *Gesammelte Schriften*, Vol. III. An English translation appeared in 1825 under the title *Memoirs of Moses Mendelssohn, the Jewish Philosopher, including the celebrated correspondence on the Christian Religion, with J. C. Lavater, Minister of Zurich, by M. Samuels.*
16. *Rome and Jerusalem*, Eng. trs. Block, 1945, pp. 156 *f*.

Chapter Six: Problems of a new Christian Attitude to Judaism

1. See, for example, the Report of the Jewish Mission Committee of the Presbyterian Church of England in Minutes of the General Assembly, 1925.
2. *The Life and Miracles of St. William of Norwich, by Thomas of Monmouth.* Ed. by A. Jessopp and M. R. James, Cambridge, 1896.
3. See *My Reminiscences*, Dr. Joseph Bloch, Vienna, 1923, Part 2, pp. 361 *ff*.
4. *Ep. ad Universos Fideles* of Pope John XX, Mansi, XXV, c. 569.
5. See *L'Apocalypse de Notre Temps*, Henri Rollin, Paris, 1939. The references to Dr. de Cyon are scattered through the book. See especially Chap. 13.
6. See, for example, introduction to Part Three.

GENERAL INDEX

INDEX OF BIBLICAL QUOTATIONS